A wonderful read. True life, tru
self-survival.

James McDonald, Psychologist, Minister

Borderline portrays reality of life here in Brewster County; the characters, settings, conflicts and resolutions described with brutal honesty and vivid poetry. It is a timely story, well told.

Perry Lee Little, Brewster Country Resident

Borderline is a guidebook on how to survive trauma and learn to prepare and prevent future trauma. As a child abuse forensic Pediatrician in a previous life, I feel this would be an excellent resource for counselors and nurses.

David Hardy MD

This is an extraordinary book about the author's life in West Texas. Jayson shares her remarkable story, from the terror of being kidnapped and raped through her struggles to regain a life with her son in a community she loves, and finally to the joy of falling in love.

KS Richter, BA, University of Texas

Borderline is a book about survival under the most harrowing conditions. A woman alone faces a ruthless stranger in a remote area, who is determined to control, dehumanize her. Jayson's courage and survival reveal an inner strength that assists her in coming through the ordeal a stronger person. This book should be made available to every crisis center nationwide.

Rod Odem, Principal (Ret)

Borderline

A true story of courage and justice

JAYSON WOODWARD

Disclaimer:
Every effort has been made to ensure this book is as accurate and complete as possible. However, there may be mistakes both typographical and in content. Therefore, this book should be used as a general guide and not and the ultimate source of information contained herein. The author and publisher shall not be liable or responsible to any person or entity with respect to any loss or damage caused or alleged to have been caused directly or indirectly by the information contained in this book.

Published by: Jayson Woodward
www.AuthorityAuthors.com.au
QLD 4019, Australia

Cover design by Independent Ink
Edited by Deirdre Swanney
Internal design by Independent Ink
Typeset in 11/15.5 pt Goudy Old Style by Post Pre-press Group, Brisbane

ISBN: 978 0 5785 2422 1

A catalogue record for this
book is available from the
National Library of Australia

This book is dedicated to all the courageous women who take upon themselves the responsibility of their own safety, who refuse to be victims, and who help others understand the importance of self protection.

Contents

Foreword

IT HAS TAKEN ME YEARS to evolve to the point of overcoming my fears of telling this story. For awhile I tried to miniaturize the impact it had on my life. For awhile I tried to "get over it." For a long time I asked, "why me? Why was I the one to suffer this incident? Why was I the one to have to fight through it? Why was I the one who had to figure it all out?" And then I began to slowly recognize, "Why NOT me?" And with that realization I started the journey of learning a new way of recognizing my own responsibility to myself. I began to learn to act in ways that honored and protected who I am. I began to love myself enough to be able to become my own guardian. I owed it to myself to try to become my best self every day.

There are many resources to help victims of crimes and their families. First and foremost, if you are a crime victim don't be afraid to reach out to your local law enforcement and report the crime. Many victims fear they will not be believed, or are embarrassed, or believe they are somehow at fault and fail to report the crime. Law enforcement officers are trained to help you.

They are well aware of local resources for your healing and will provide the information you need. While you may be hesitant to relate the event you have suffered, don't be embarrassed ... there is nothing they have not already heard.

There are many avenues to take to begin and to further your healing. There are techniques you can train yourself to use that will lower your stress levels, intervene in the constant review of the horrific events you suffered, and to lessen the anger you may feel. There are counseling centers that will help you, and any family members affected.

The last page of this book has a listing of resources that you can contact. Once you reach out for help you will find many, many more paths to take to help you regain your health and sense of safety.

The hard work of "becoming" is constant, a never receding act of try and try again. Once you know, you can't NOT know. Turns out, holding oneself accountable is the highest act of love. If you are a victim, reach out to the resources you have that will enable you to become whole.

Jayson

1

Finding West Texas

It's not like they tell you it would be, or even how you expected it to be, this changing, this becoming a different person. D.H. Lawrence said something like, "It is not easy to change. You must first pass through the waters of oblivion." Sometimes it starts off slow. You may feel a little discomfort, a feeling that something isn't quite right. Sometimes it slams you in the face, so obvious you lose your breath. Sometimes you choose to change. Sometimes change chooses you. This book is about how I experienced both. Reliving it all becomes the last flickering memory of yourself before the erasure of oblivion sets in.

It was summer and Trey and I were falling in love. A rancher's eldest son, he was in charge while his mother, Pattie, was miles away in El Paso, dying of cancer, with his father, Frank, by her side. A seeming miracle had brought me to his family's ranch, an oasis set in the middle of the largest county in Texas, replete with sunrises and sunsets that colored the world in hues of orange, pink and purple. A bad divorce and the need to completely cut my ex-husband out of my life had taken me through Central America for four years. As my son neared school age my journey had spit me out in West Texas and ultimately led me directly to the ranch known for hiring strays and wayward souls – Woodward Ranch.

One of my earliest memories was of a children's book about a little girl who saw a little boy at a circus, all dressed in cowboy clothes, standing in the glow of sunset. She walked up to him and held his hand while, as they say, "the sun sank slowly in the west", with circus tents behind them. I hadn't thought of it in years but it must have been branded into my memory, because the minute I saw Trey, I saw that little boy. I was Home.

Trey was just my type of guy. Polite like only a west Texas man can be, with an honest grin that said, "I'm a nice guy not a player." At the ripe old age of 30 I recognized him to be unlike any of the boyfriends of my past. A bit shy, he took his time to start a conversation, but if he liked you, you knew it immediately. True to my '70s roots and budding interest in astrology, I chalked it all up to him being a Cancer, with its traditional values of loyalty, truthfulness, kindness, and being a mate-for-life kind of guy.

Growing up on the ranch suited him perfectly. He sometimes had a hard time blending in to the world around him, but the ranch was his kingdom. And once he fell in love, he stayed in love. His face told the whole story. Electric blue eyes and a face of soft contours, it was easy to read the "love at first sight" melting of his heart. He had a way of inviting you into his life, and if you ventured to go, he held you fast. I wanted to be held fast. I wanted a home.

The ranch was not just a working cattle ranch. It was a geological paradise. Over 50 different kinds of agate could be found there, along with opal, labradorite, and quartz. Visitors came from all over the world to hunt the gemstones, see the rock shop, and bask in the calm quiet of nature.

The rock shop had exquisite specimens of all the stones that could be found on the ranch, as well as a collection of incredible rocks from around the world. Frank was a geologist by trade, and a thorough, if not compassionate, teacher by heart. On his good days he would hold court on the geology of the ranch and how the minerals had been formed. He taught me how to change the rough rocks into polished and smooth beauties that were then fashioned into unique items of jewelry. I taught myself how to arrange the inventory to be most appealing to the customers. I loved every aspect of the business of the ranch.

The tourists who visited the ranch kept Trey, his siblings and me busy. Between the five of us, Trey, Mark, Emily, David and me, we were barely able to hit all the bases. The tourists either rented a cabin by the creek or camped in tents. The ranch was known for its hospitality to everyone, offering not just recreation, but the experience of long-gone days of open friendliness to anyone who happened by. More often than not, there would be "extras" for lunch or dinner, as tourists were unaccustomed to being so far away from restaurants or grocery stores and arrived unprepared for a longer stay. During the "busy season" the chores stretched endlessly throughout the day and into the evening. Meals had to be made, the shop had to be cleaned and kept tidy, tourists had to be shown where and how to hunt for the gemstones, their collected bounty had to be explained to them when they returned from their hunt, the cows and horses had to be fed. And of course, each and every guest had to be accounted for each and every day. With over two thousand acres, we had to keep up with the general area the guests would be rock hunting in, and make sure they arrived back at headquarters before dark. When they didn't, Trey and I would seize the opportunity to jump into his truck and, "go looking". That was a quaint euphemism for driving through the ranch at twilight, taking our time, stopping for long pauses, ostensibly to "listen for the hunters". We were nothing if not thorough, sometimes arriving home well past dark. But, like shepherds, we always brought back the guests.

In our "spare" time, when Frank was back from El Paso, he taught me how to use the grinders, tumblers, polishers, engravers, and how to make jewelry out of the fabulous stones. While making beautiful jewelry he taught me the characteristics of different gemstones. The hardness of the stone, the differences in clarity, and the uniqueness of one stone not found anywhere but on the ranch; red plume agate. There was really no end to it and I found it all fascinating. But with Pattie gone and Frank only home sporadically, the workload more than doubled for everyone. That hardly mattered to us. We were young and had boundless energy. We were in love and consumed with the ecstatic fire one finds in a first true love. We were blessed.

If there was one song that characterized that long summer it was Leon Russell's "Back to the Island". The ranch, miles away from any town, was an island unto itself. Mountains, creeks, rocky pastures and giant cottonwood trees formed the backdrop for two young lovers to find each other. Even though it was left unsaid, Trey and I both knew his mother wouldn't last long. To keep our minds off that we rode horses, fed cows, cooked food, worked the garden and took care of the younger kids, Mark, Emily, David and little Holly, Trey's niece and companion to my son, Noah. We lived on our own island with summer thunderstorms so magnificent they took your breath right out of your chest, and cool clear nights that only a high desert climate can bring.

Trey and I had a saying. "The summer days blaze, but the nights are hot." We slept on the screened-in porch of his grandfather's house, letting those night breezes wash over us in waves ... like the ocean. We'd stay up most of the night, laughing, loving, and looking out at the sheer emptiness of the ranch. No lights, no sound, no people. Just us, and like twenty-somethings do, no plans, no cares, no worries. We stretched out the summer in a blissful present tense.

There was real work to be done, too. With Trey's parents gone I handled the rock shop, the house and the cooking while Trey and his two brothers took care of the ranch and the cows. It was all so new and exciting for a city girl. The round up, the branding, separating the calves from their mothers, castrating the males so they wouldn't grow into bulls. On roundup days, Trey's friends and a few guys from nearby ranches would show up early. They'd saddle their horses and ride out to search every pasture for cows. Usually by noon they would come riding slowly back behind the cows, pushing the herd into the pens by the big rock barn. After watering their horses and tying them in the shade, the guys would wash up and head for the dinner table.

I was lucky. My mother had taught me to cook the way her mother had taught her to cook. I remember as a child standing on a chair in front of the stove and getting to stir what she said to stir, or mash what she said to mash. I watched her every move, and now it served me well. But being young and inexperienced in cooking for more than three or four folks I had to adapt to the demand. I'd look for menu items that could be made ahead of time, or at least a few that could be, leaving the main items for the last minute. We often had pinto beans, fried chicken, mashed potatoes and usually coleslaw and hot cornbread. There had to be ice tea, and the ranch well water made the best I had ever tasted before or since. For dessert, something easy, like cowboy cobbler or sometimes banana pudding. Trey's sister, Emily, would usually help in the kitchen, even though her preference was to be out brushing the horses down. Or lovingly talking to them. Or feeding them apples. At 14, her whole world was horses. And they loved her as much as she did them.

After the morning round up, the real work in the pens would begin. Calves would be separated by age and size and branded or castrated. It was dusty, dirty and sweaty work, and the tequila bottle was passed around all afternoon until the job was finished. Then the help would leave, the horses fed and brushed, and the gates of the pens opened for the mother cows to lead their calves back out to pasture. All in a day's work. That was the life Trey relished, and one I was quickly learning to love.

Even though we knew it couldn't last forever and that change was surely coming, the thought was still just out of reach of real consciousness. Our thoughts were fixed on the present day to day running of the ranch. There wasn't time to plan or prepare for the future.

Late that summer Trey's mother and father returned to the ranch. The doctors in El Paso could do nothing else for Pattie, and the next two weeks or so were a dark introduction of how short life is. Ranch work came to a standstill but the rock shop stayed open. Frank handled that just to stay busy and to forget, if only for a little while, that his wife was dying. The rest of us stayed close to the house, trying to be useful, trying to be upbeat, trying not to focus on what was coming. Pattie died peacefully, surrounded by her husband, children, and the animals she loved, including Flicka, a white-tail deer she had raised from its birth.

Even though Flicka was wild, she had the run of the house. A small towel was tied to the front screen door and Flicka could pull on it, open the door, and trot right in to the house. A drawer in the kitchen was Flicka's drawer. The handle tied with another towel, Flicka would pull on the drawer to reveal an open bag of her favorite ... marshmallows! She would eat her fill, then trot out the backscreen door to continue feasting on her more regular fare. No one had seen Flicka in almost 2 years, and most of the family had decided, regretfully, that Flicka had forgotten all about them and her marshmallows. But as Pattie lay in bed dying, Flicka appeared outside her bedroom door. And she wasn't alone. She had brought her twin fawns with her! Twins are highly unusual in the wild animal world, and we were all amazed. Flicka stood there at Pattie's door, as if to say goodbye to the friend who had raised her those many years earlier. Pattie broke into a grin that we had not seen on her in weeks, and for a few hours, experienced a comfort she had almost forgotten as she battled the cancer that was so incessant. All of us stood there smiling through our tears, but not unaccustomed to the small miracles we had all seen on the ranch. It was a special place and a special time, almost a moment out of time. And then just as suddenly as she had appeared, Flicka and her fawns bounded away. We never saw them again.

Trey and his siblings were still so young, and the very thought of being without a mother was a frightening and incomprehensible idea. We all tried to carry on to keep everything as "normal" as we could, if not for ourselves, then for Pattie. When it was over, and after Pattie had been laid to rest, we all tried our best to regain our balance and resume the rhythm of the ranch. But it was no use. With Pattie's absence everything shifted. The change slammed us in the face, and then began its unalterable settling into our lives.

Frank resumed his heavy handed, narcissistic power. He still disapproved of me, putting Trey in the position of having to defy his father to be with the one he loved. Our intuition told us that everything was rapidly becoming something else, and our world would be different, so we tried to live every moment of the present like the gift it was. It made Leon Russel's song all the more important to us ... the waves of the song's ocean moving in and out, the separation we knew was coming, the background of almost holy singers ... the combination kept us clinging to each other trying to ward off the end that was charging straight at us.

Of course, we couldn't have possibly known the full extent of the changes that would come, or how Pattie's death would produce the prolonged pause that would affect us, our families, our friends, and a few people in Mexico. Looking back on that summer I can see it hung heavy with a promise that would, in the end, force all of us to believe in the wonder of life and the sometimes brutal magic of love.

2

A Feeling Not a Place

PATTIE'S DEATH WAS BOTH A tragedy and, sadly, a kind of blessing. She had battled cancer so long and so bravely. She had one of the sweetest personalities I had ever encountered. Always kind to strays of any kind, animals or humans, she offered her home as a safe haven. She had a way with wild animals. She rescued a baby javelina who was orphaned, and as it grew up, it never left her side. It even slept by her in bed! Soft-spoken and kind, her life on the ranch had been hard.

Even though she was only fifty, she had suffered longer than anyone knew, and from maladies more than just the cancer. Her husband Frank was a complicated man, and selfish to boot. Through the years his heavy-handed domination created more rebellion than anything else. But having been in a sense excommunicated from my own birth family, I was hungry for the love and acceptance of a close family unit, and, at the beginning, fairly blind to any harshness I saw coming from Frank. I saw him then as a commanding head of the household doing all he could to hold his family, and the ranch, together. At times he had a great sense of humor, and at times he seemed a genius with all the geology he knew. He was also well versed in history, and had been an officer in the Air Force. He was everything my own father wasn't. Where my father was unforgiving and unaccepting of anything not decreed by him to be okay, Frank chalked misdeeds up to human nature and forgot about them. One of his favorite sayings was, "Just look at their pointy heads and forgive them." My father was steeped in a middleclass existence of making money and keeping up with the Joneses, whereas Frank could not have cared less what anyone thought of him. Since I hadn't grown up with Frank as my father, I didn't see the darker side of him. I saw only what I needed to see at the time, and what I needed was to feel a part of family.

I didn't see the dark side then, but my judgement now is harsh at best. I came to understand that at times Frank seemed to be different personalities: caring and sympathetic one minute, loud and demanding the next. You were never quite sure where you really stood with him and that instability eventually grew into the "walking on eggshells" syndrome that most abused people learn.

Dealing with Frank, caring for five children, and living in the isolation of the ranch, Pattie had learned to put up with just about anything. As was common with wives in that day, her husband's rule was law, and Frank had plenty of rules. His main rule was that the world revolved around him. Having grown up with the narcissism of my own father, that didn't seem strange to me.

Due to his many eccentricities Frank was never really respected by other ranchers in the area. He dominated his children, and his wife, and the isolation of the ranch ensured he could act out in ways unacceptable to the "ordinary" folk of the county. With all his faults, he held himself in high esteem, if only to demean others. Eventually, I was no exception.

I was not the picture of the wife he expected for his eldest son. I had been previously married and had a young son. I was almost

9 years older than Trey. I was not easy to control. I was smart. Pretending to like me, Frank would find subtle ways to make sure I knew he didn't approve of my relationship with Trey. "If the milk is free, why buy the cow?" he would often remark, sneering at me as if I were sullied material.

By his 20s Trey was already an alcoholic. He drank to ease the long days of work on the ranch. He drank to forget his father's abuse. He drank to irritate Frank. He drank because when it was time to relax that was the only way he knew how. Until the magic of our first summer he drank every day. But that long and beautiful summer with Pattie and Frank gone, Trey had begun to find himself. He saw that as far as running the ranch, he was more capable than his father. His younger siblings respected him, and worked hard to gain his praise or recognition. For once, everyone was happy. And for once, without Frank's violent outbursts, no one was scared. We all relished the freedom.

But after Pattie's death and Frank's return to the ranch everything again disintegrated into chaos. Frank was in mourning, displaying grief and anger. Trey was overwhelmed and drinking heavier than ever. Frank's earlier attempts at demeaning me became more blatant and more frequent, in my estimation to the point of being dangerous. It was hard for me to watch the way he bullied Mark, the way he groomed Emily to be subservient to him, the way he tore down any self-confidence Trey had attained. As each day passed it grew more apparent that he did not want me on the ranch. I was in his way. With the situation so toxic I had begun to feel the same way Frank did ... I needed to leave.

Trey couldn't come with me. The ranch was now hundreds of thousands of dollars in debt due to Pattie's illness and hospitalization. Frank was dependent upon Trey to pull the ranch out of debt, even though he constantly berated and denigrated him.

And, as all abuse victims are, Trey was tied to that role and his father's demands in spite of knowing he was giving up his own hopes and dreams. It was really too sad to watch.

Then, as sometimes happens in life when an impasse occurs, the universe offers up its own solution. And, as often happens, when presented with a fork in the road, the path not taken makes all the difference. I was offered a good job in a neighboring town about eighty miles away. Eighty miles away *south* of the ranch, toward the Texas/Mexico border. The pay was excellent and there was a local school for my son. How could I say no? We both believed that eighty miles was not an insurmountable distance and we would still be together. And in that assumption, we both forgot about the power of growth, evolution, and the steady winds of change that life brings. We were too young to know that life *is* change. Life is dynamic, not static. We both had a lot of growing to do. We decided that what we had was a feeling, not a place, and that we would still be together, just miles apart. And so, I left and Trey stayed. And it would be years before we would meet again, and under circumstances we could not have imagined.

3

Into the Wild

MY NEW JOB WAS AT a small 4th-class post office in an area known as Terlingua. 100 miles or so south of the nearest town of Alpine, Terlingua itself was a barely populated ghost town. It had a 4th-grade post office, and I was the only employee, the Postmaster. While it served a huge area, there were only about 300 people in the area who actually had a mailbox in the post office. There was no delivery to individual residents, and my official job was to sort the mail that arrived once a day, sell money orders and stamps, place people's mail in their respective mailboxes, and receive outgoing mail for the following day. But unofficially, I was news central for the whole area. Since I saw and talked with everyone almost every day, I had all the news that was "fit to print." And, as the area drew more and more tourists, I became a sort of unofficial tourist bureau. Visitors would stop, not only to have their mail stamped with the increasingly popular "Terlingua" post stamp, but to get information on the area, its history, and what it had to offer. And that led to my second job, that of tourist guide for the first, and at that time only, "resort".

In the early days, the area had been a booming mining endeavor, until the need for cinnabar, quick silver, became obsolete ... like the buggy whip. Dotted for miles with rock ruins of pitiful dwellings the early miners had to endure, the area itself sat at the western entrance of what was now Big Bend National Park, offering a few bare tourist amenities until people could get back to civilization. There was a small grocery store, Study Butte Porch, that doubled as one of the few places folks could gather that offered shade, a gas station, a couple of cafes, and a refurbished mine known as Villa de la Mina that could house and feed twenty or so tourists at a time, with plenty of space for bigger events. Owned by Glen and Donna Pepper, the Villa de la Mina was the first real accommodation to be opened for tourists. They had restored four of the rock ruins on the property to be comfortable, if quaint, cabins for tourists. Each cabin had a bathroom and was furnished with "Tex-Mex" amenities, just the feel that tourists were looking for. The largest cabin had a full kitchen and a modern "sunken" living room that could accommodate a larger crowd.

The Peppers' house had once been the main office of the mining company. With beautiful Mexican tile floors and large airy rooms, their living room became the lobby for guests, and opened up into a stunning plant room hewed out of the cliff behind the house. With water slowly misting out of the native rock walls, the plants offered a cool oasis for their guests. And the accommodations included one evening meal, masterfully prepared by Donna, and served buffet style in the dining room adjacent to the lobby.

Behind the house and approximately fifty yards down a rock road, lay the entrance to the old mine. A crude string of lights stretched from its entrance down the main tunnel for several hundred feet. One of my jobs was to take tourists into the mine to get a firsthand look at the geology of the area, and to see the cinnabar still embedded in the rock. The main tunnel eventually opened into a large cavern maybe seventy-five feet high. Stalactites of quartz pointed like arrows from the top of the cave. The sides were striped with veins of rust red cinnabar, quartz and calcite. You felt like you were standing inside a geode. It was magnificent, and the tourists were always audibly amazed. The mine stayed at a constant temperature of seventy-two degrees. Pepper tried for years to devise a way to pipe the cool mine air into the main house for a respite from the tortuous desert heat. It never actually happened, but remained a constant source of conversation as tourists and workers alike sat at the big picnic table on the front porch to mull over this and other weighty matters.

"The Villa" as the locals called it, was one of three establishments to have a telephone. Study Butte porch on the east edge of the area had a phone, The Villa on the southwestern edge, and in between the two was Carolina White's small convenience store with telephone service. The phone lines back then stretched the hundred miles or so from Alpine across the tops of fence posts. If the wind blew, as it often did, or it rained, which was seldom, or if the sun rose on alternate Tuesdays, the phone lines would go down. The whole area encompassed maybe sixty or seventy miles of vacant terrain, with no police station, no Sheriff's deputies, and only 1 constable. And that, in itself, was enough of a draw to bring various "characters" to South County, as the general area was called.

With miles and miles of empty desert, only one paved road, subsistence housing, and little communication with the outside world, South County had earned a reputation of being a hard scrabble area that drew not only out-of-the-ordinary folks, but a few criminals as well. Most residents in the more populated towns of Brewster County, Alpine or Marathon, thought of the area as a home for hippies, miscreants and alcoholics. Being right on the southern border, it was also a gateway for illegal drugs and people.

It had just the right amount of danger and excitement that any self-respecting tourist craved.

Life in Terlingua, for the few full-timers who lived there year-round, was laid back and easy going. Winters were marked by the November International Chili Cook-Off held at the Villa de la Mina. With a crazy conglomerate of Dallas socialites, cowboys, chili companies, Willie Nelson, and cops, thousands of people would descend on an area the size of a few acres to drink, listen and dance to good Texas music, watch wet T-shirt contests, buy various and sundry items they didn't need, and eat chili. One of the biggest, if not THE biggest public party in Texas, Terlingua was quickly gaining notoriety. Every year brought the crazy antics of people who felt invincible so far away from home. It seemed that every law enforcement officer in Texas wanted to be assigned duty to the cook-off. Texas Rangers, Sheriff's departments, Department of Public Safety officers, D.E.A., Border Patrol, Constables and who knows what other law enforcement agencies were represented every year. And every local resident who was getting by without a driver's license, mandatory insurance, or a registered vehicle knew to stay home during the annual event.

Without a proper jail, the Villa de la Mina had to find a place for those arrested until law enforcement had a large enough "load" to transport to the jail in Alpine. Usually the overly exuberant and intoxicated law breakers were simply handcuffed and placed in the back of a pickup truck parked on the ridge by Pepper's house where law enforcement stood surveying the crowd below. There was one particular occasion when everyone, including law enforcement, had a good laugh.

It was during the years when "streaking" had become all the rage. Almost every televised football game had a fan who would strip down to his birthday suit and run across the field. The

Chili Cook-off was no exception. One highly intoxicated young man, without a stitch of clothes on, ran through the crowd below the ridge where law enforcement officers were standing. At first a couple of officers started to leave and chase down the brazen law breaker, but then realized he was heading straight up the ridge to the line of officers. They simply waited for him to top the ridge and run into them, red-rover style. He was handcuffed and placed, completely naked, in the back of the pickup truck. Suddenly sober, he begged the officers for his clothes or a least a towel to cover himself. The officers refused and for the rest of the night he was on display for anyone who cared to walk by the truck. He became part of the entertainment for that night, and a Chili Cook-off legend.

Summers drifted by, marked by the lack of enthusiasm for anything that required movement. South County was not like the ranch. Lower in elevation, summer temperatures could reach one hundred and twenty-five degrees or better. My feet would burn on the top due to the high temperature of the ground. With very little shade, the few residents who stayed throughout the summer adopted the Mexican time table ... up early, back inside by noon, out again around 3 or 4 o'clock, then busy 'til late.

"Busy" in Terlingua could be translated as "party time". There was always a campfire somewhere with home-grown musicians, lots of alcohol, plenty of smoke, and tall tales ... made up or real. With no city light pollution within four hundred miles, the Milky Way stretched like a lighted skyway bridge across the heavens, and every star in the universe twinkled in its dazzling best. In those days we weren't bothered with anything electronic. With no television or radio signals, and only the 3 telephones to connect us to the outside world, life was ours to craft. We wrote our own songs, made up our own stories, found ways to make our own fun.

With the Rio Grande river only about 17 miles to the south, river rafting was becoming the best way to lure tourists to the area. Pepper's Villa de la Mina offered the first commercial river trips in south county, and I was lucky enough to moonlight on some of them. Widely acclaimed as the most scenic canyon of the river was Santa Elena Canyon. One night, while trying to gather the tourists at the pickup location, I was stranded on the wrong side of Terlingua Creek. It had been raining hard and the river was running high. All the creeks had "come down" and Terlingua Creek was raging. Knowing that Terlingua Creek would run down eventually, I sat in the van and wrote a song about it until the early hours of the morning. By the time I got to the tourists at the takeout point, they all had a story they could tell their grandchildren. So did I.

SANTA ELENA CANYON
We watched the sky the day it rained,
heavy clouds gathered up in the south.
It was early in April and not many folks
Really thought we should worry about
the way the air grew thick, your breathin'
grew tough.

It was enough to make you choke
We sat uneasy and waited and watched
The desert has damn few jokes.

I was sittin' at the bottom of Santa Elena Canyon,
Those walls rose sheer to the sky.
We could reach high ground if we all had wings
But no one wanted to try.

And the Rio Grande mud, thick as blood,
While the wind began to howl.
The current so fast, and nuthin' to sink
And them dark pools whirlin' around.

I've seen grown men cry, I've heard a bird scream
Seen enough in my life for ten.
But nothing like the sound, it turned my soul around,
When Terlingua Creek roared in.

The months and seasons drifted by in the easy sustained feeling of youth, before realizing that time is not infinite. I saw Trey again only twice during the next several years. Once he was dead drunk at a party in one of the arroyos near the Study Butte Porch. I couldn't even speak to him. The next time was at a Chili Cook-off. Drunk again, but still able to stand up, he hugged me and said hello. We both had tears in our eyes.

And so, the loneliness of leaving Trey and the ranch was slowly consumed by working, raising Noah and part time work with the Villa de la Mina. I ran for the school board and won. I helped raise money for the EMS and volunteer fire department. I did all the things small town folks do to pass the time profitably and try to make a difference in their communities.

Not surprisingly, living over one hundred miles away from the nearest town (and a small one at that), even mundane chores took an inordinate amount of time. About once every 3 weeks or so, I'd make the drive into town for groceries and a taste of west Texas "civilization". There was 1 grocery store, Safeway, 2 clothing stores, Anthony's and Forsheimer's, a few gas stations, and the Hut, where you could buy the best hamburger this side of the Pecos River. Usually it was at least an all-day affair, and sometimes I'd stay overnight so that I could take my time and leisurely make the drive back to Terlingua, slowly breathing in the beauty of the vast Chihuahuan desert.

The majesty of the Big Bend area always overwhelmed me. Just being a small part so it was like living a prayer. About 20 miles outside of Alpine you pass Cathedral Mountain, where the praying begins. Everything up to that point is only beautiful. But the prayer begins in earnest at Cathedral, as you drive down the last rise, take the last curve where everything is still green. Then you're headed due south and the rugged landscape unfolds in front of you like an apron. The fabric is every tone of the earth, every shade of brown, yellow, red, violet, blue, and white of the spectrum. The chalk dust overlay gives it the look of a watercolor. The two-lane highway is a rough gray tongue and you slide for maybe eighty miles before you hit the edge of the Chisos Mountains. The "Ghost Mountains" the Apache named them, and you didn't have to be there long to find out why.

The years rolled on, time slipping away like it always does. Even now I can feel the hold of its magic. There was a time I thought I would never leave; a time when I couldn't imagine myself ever wanting to be away from the timeless moment of the desert. And then there came a time when I had given up all hope of ever getting away from the desert's grasp. Those were the days when I had become "un-matter", a true daughter of the Chisos. A wisp of nothing, disappeared into my own hell.

4

Comanche Moon

SOMETIMES I STILL THINK ABOUT those two hours just before the "big catastrophe". Coming home from a two-day town trip, all the groceries being carted in and set among the leavings of a hasty departure of two days earlier, there was plenty to do. Put groceries away, unpack, empty the ice chest, plenty to do to fill up a lonely Saturday night. Noah was gone for the weekend to overnight at a friend's house. I had the whole evening to myself. The whole, quiet, evening. Everything was so quiet. Even my cats were gone. It felt a bit strange ... they should be clawing their way into the new bag of cat chow by now. But those were just fleeting thoughts. After the long drive home, I wasn't ready to do any work. Not yet. I decided to walk across the patio to my bedroom, to count out the Mexican pesos I planned to exchange the next day in Lajitas when I would pick Noah up from his friend's house. Sitting there counting the money, I was surprised to see I had nearly $60. I could use the money.

And then the thoughts stopped. The conversation in my head stopped. Everything stopped and there was only the quiet, the quiet feeling that I was being watched. The back of my neck felt tight and prickly. Sweat broke out on my face. I sat still, moving only my eyes across the room without raising my head, sure that I would find someone standing there. Not even daring to breathe, my eyes swept the bedroom and sitting room. There was no one there and I heaved a sigh of relief. "You're scaring yourself," I thought, "feeling sorry for yourself because you're here alone and all your friends are at the dance in Lajitas." The conversation in my head started up again.

Lajitas, a small resort community about 20 miles away, was known for its monthly dances that proved to be the biggest event of any season. Local or regional bands would play, and people from all over the six thousand square miles of Brewster County would come, as well as anyone from Mexico who could walk, swim, or take the little boat across the Rio Grande. In the best Texas tradition, it was a melting pot of generations and cultures. Parents, kids, grandparents, anyone who could walk attended, if not to dance, then to meet old friends, or make new ones, drink beer, gossip and forget about daily cares.

Too tired to get ready and go to the dance to "see and be seen", I decided to entertain myself by playing my guitar and singing my newest songs. It always helps to sing. And so, I sat on the deck and sang to the sunset. I sang until I was hoarse. I poured my heart out to the empty evening. Stopping to put my guitar away and get some water, the conversation in my head started up again.

"Go to the kitchen and get a drink. Better yet, just go. Get in your truck and go to the dance. Well ... maybe ... but no. I'd have to get changed and ... then just get in your truck. Go as you are and just drive around. Just get in your truck." The conversation, unbidden, was becoming weird. Sure, I talked to myself now and then, but this seemed different. The voice was somewhat strident, and issuing the same message over and over. "Go. Get in your truck. Leave."

I needed water. I walked into my kitchen off the deck and drank a big glass of ice-cold water. It cleared my head, and stopped the conversation with myself long enough to remember that tonight was a full moon. Glancing out the window I could see it was just beginning to get dark. It was to be a Comanche moon, one of the year's biggest, and I walked back out onto the deck so as not to miss a moment of its rising.

Standing there in the stunning orange glow of the rising moon was magnificent. I was enveloped in a quiet so deep it was palpable, a feast for the senses. It was the last time I would feel that peaceful and safe for the next 20 years.

5

Back to Alpine

THE FIRST FEW HOURS AFTER it was over (I thought then it was over, but no, it goes on and on, even today), a calm clarity seemed to settle over me, paralyzing my body, and making my thoughts the only reality I experienced. I had a vision of myself as being very large, and round, puffed up, almost like that Comanche moon as it peeked out over the horizon, while the stillness and the emptiness surrounded me. All of me was large, and quiet, and vacant, with the only sound a sustained bass note that one would associate with dawn.

And, in fact, it was dawn. The endless stretch of miles in a desert dawn is beautiful. The blackness of the last lingering of night gradually painted the sky with shell colors. The sound and the colors made my roundness and vacancy seem so still. And just before the sun was really up, in that suspended moment when everything blazes gold, before the light actually transforms the desert to day, it was then that I knew. I knew without analysis or contemplation or carefully worded conversation with myself, knew without fear, or anxiety, knew without reserving even the tiniest place of retreat, that everything I had ever been, the sum of all my parts, all of my known world, had somehow been erased ... terminated. There was not even the memory of who I had been. There was only the color of the dawn and the sound of the note, and the desert landscape falling, falling away from me.

By the time we got to town it was the full light of day. And it was ugly. Town streets are always the same gray asphalt, the buildings stabbing the sky, and everything connected to everything else by the unending black cable, strung from raw pillar to raw pillar, like some grotesque Christmas tree tinsel. Utility poles are castrated trees, splintery and denuded, silent guardians of progress. That's what it is about towns; they give you the *feeling* of time. And suddenly you find yourself compartmentalizing everything, assigning this and allotting that. The sheer ugliness brought me back to the present.

By the time we backed up to the emergency room entrance of the hospital I again felt the terror of the preceding hours. Completely deflated now, feeling small and out of place, I was terrified at the twenty or so faces looking in from the outside, framed by the rear windows of the ambulance doors. I wondered what they were waiting for and why they looked to be so intense, so concentrated? I had forgotten the nurse sitting beside me long ago, miles ago. Her incessant questions had faded and finally blended into the bass tone, and I remember how the tears spilling out of her eyes had been absorbed and become a part of the desert dew that helped to polish that sparkling moment, just before dawn. "Don't you want to get out now?" I heard her gently ask in an attempt to dislodge me from the stretcher.

I told her I would, if all of the people staring at me would leave. I don't know how she made it happen, but the people parted and left enough room for me to step out of the ambulance and walk through the wide doors into a bright and polished hallway. And then they closed around me as a group, telling me who they were and how they were going to assist me, leading me into a small exam room. A new nurse entered, along with a doctor, and helped me get onto the examining table. I seemed to move in slow motion, and followed their instructions without really hearing them, relying on their gestures to show me what to do. My mind didn't work, my ears didn't work, my words didn't work and I felt as if I could sleep for days. Exhausted as I was, the examining table looked pretty inviting. I was wrong.

6

Hospital

A RAPE EXAM IS NOT like anything else. Even though you're a grown woman (And how many times have you been on that table?) and well used to those cold steel stirrups and the hard, little padding layered with some non-distinct-brown shade of plastic, overlaid again with the white, crackling paper, even so, it doesn't seem all right. I know what they are going to do, but they tell me first anyway. It still doesn't seem all right. But I've had a baby, and bladder infections and IUDs and pap smears before, and after the first time, you don't usually cry. I remember to remind myself that I don't cry anymore at such indignities. And the two nurses, and the counselors, and the doctor are all talking, their words and bodies taking up what tiny little space there was in the room.

Someone takes my hand and tells me it will all be over in just a minute. Of course, I know that. Somehow the words push me into remembering my mother's funeral, and how everyone stood around looking uncomfortable but trying to be cheery. They might as well have said, "Well, and yes, she's dead and all that, but this will all be over soon." I imagine my mother lying in her casket and thinking, "Well, of course. I know that."

So, with all the probing, and talking, hand-holding, and flash-backing I was totally unprepared for whatever apparatus the doctor plunged into my rectum. It hurt, and the pain and the suddenness jerked me back to before the dawn, long before the dawn. And then I do cry and I can't stop and when I hear the doctor say nonchalantly that there is gravel and dirt and "fluids", the cries turn by themselves to sobs and the sobs to wracking, uncontrollable shuddering. I can't stop and the nurse bends onto my chest, mixing her tears with mine, and begs over and over how it "won't be long".

Like several frames left out of a movie, everything becomes calm and still again. No more sobs and no more pain, and the doctor instructs the nurse to give me penicillin and someone says to please roll over. Rolling over now, and staring at the floor, I see someone picking up my little heap of clothes off the floor and stuffing them into a bag. I vaguely wonder what I'll wear when I'm able to leave this stifling room.

Time speeds up again as I watch the nurse fill a huge syringe. She tells me it will hurt, but it will hurt less if I relax my muscles. And now the nurse is crying too, and hands the syringe to someone else and I have already decided it won't hurt. I won't let it hurt. Nothing will ever hurt me again.

The doctor helped me to sit up, and gave me a sympathetic look and pat on the back. One of the nurses left, and the other one asked in a bare whisper if I was ready to speak with some officers. Officers? What kind of officers I wondered? Still in a confused and dazed state, I didn't want to talk, I wanted to sleep. I was so tired of the speeded up, then slowed down, then speeded up again pace of everything, I just wanted a real bed in a dark and silent room. But being the ever-compliant Texas girl, I nodded agreement to her request, and sat up straight in the too-well-lighted room, perched like an unsure bird on the edge of the little table, legs dangling from beneath the too short and too green hospital gown. Several men dressed in different uniforms walked in, eyes downcast, not meeting my gaze. Carrying some sort of recording equipment, they arranged a small table and chairs so that they could sit down. As awkward as it was, I understood that now, now it was time to talk.

"Brewster County Memorial Hospital, treatment room 101, 9:16 a.m., 10/27/85. Those present are John Alexander, Medic; Janice K. Harvey, Director of the Brewster County Women's Shelter; Billy Pat McKinney, Constable, Precinct 2 Brewster County; Gary Richards, Deputy Sheriff. Trying to keep up with all the names, my mind was stuck on his beginning words.

As denial began to recede and clarity return, the magnitude of the previous 14 hours started to creep into my consciousness. Suddenly grateful that another woman was in the room with me, I was beginning to understand that I would have to tell them all exactly what had happened. "And thank God for Billy Pat," I thought. Being from Terlingua, he was the only one I knew. I had written a song about him. His daughter was on the school board with me. I could tell by the looks on their faces that this was as unpleasant for them as it was going to be for me.

In his best professional voice, Deputy Richards started off. "Now just go ahead and start from the beginning. Give me a date and time, and ... it's going to be just like telling a story, ok? You don't have to rush, just take your time."

Now this was beginning to feel unreal. All these people squeezed into the tiny room, watching me. The man speaking into the tape recorder, preserving for all posterity a private moment that I wished would go away. And now I'm supposed to tell the story. Nothing made sense anymore, everything was again beginning to be disconnected from everything else. I was even disconnected from myself. "Where did my beautiful desert stop and all these heavy images begin to appear? Who *is* this person perched so precariously here trying to collect her thoughts?" My mind began to flutter into a thousand disjointed pieces, all the thoughts running together.

Remember a long, long time ago when you went to the "show" (they say "movies" or "films" now) and there'd be a double feature, several cartoons, an episode of a serial, and a song, a song flashed across the screen with a white ball hopping from one word to the next? The melody would play and I guess the audience was supposed to follow the white ball and sing along, but no one ever did. Well, it was like that. All the text of my words hanging in front of me, the whole story, like laundry. But I wasn't just sitting there looking at the words. I was on the other side of them, too, looking slightly down at myself. And really, the room was so tiny, there wasn't much place to be, but I managed to be everywhere. I couldn't possibly put all the "Me"s together, and I couldn't decide which one would speak. That *was* the questions, wasn't it? Someone *did* ask me to tell a story? And then I heard my own voice, and the other parts of me, sitting like a gallery, we were amazed. Amazed not so much by what was being said, but at the strange editing process of the speaker and what was being left unsaid.

The other voices in my head muttered, "She forgot to tell them how beautiful the desert looked, standing there on the deck by the cactus garden. She didn't tell them how it gets dark pretty late and there's a point when half the sky is ink and the other half, the half to the west, is still only gray, with the last light sinking. And the moon ... oh the full moon in the desert! How can I tell them how beautiful it was, standing there in the deepest quiet, watching the moonlight make the desert dance with the clearest, softest glow? And then suddenly it isn't quiet anymore. And my scream is piercing the night, and I am in a million pieces, shattered, and scattered everywhere in a jumbled confusion. His arm is across my throat, tighter, tighter, and his hand is over my mouth and something sharp sticks into my neck. All of my pieces are sending separate messages: this isn't happening. This is just someone's idea of a joke. You are dreaming. Why does it smell like ivory soap? You're being pulled backwards. I didn't know you could understand Spanish! Where did he come from? It was so quiet! Why didn't you hear, why didn't you hear?"

And then, standing outside myself, I am looking only at my own eyes. They are huge and round, and they seem to be as big as the world, and hollow. Gaping holes staring, staring at the night.

7

The Recount

"Now, Ma'm, I know this is hard for you, but if you could just pick up where you left off, and we'll go on with the story. "The deputy spoke in a soft and polite voice. "Can you go on?" His question jerked me out of my thoughts and brought me back to the tight little room. "Oh. Oh, I thought I was talking," I managed to stammer, "but I guess I was lost in thought."

"That's certainly understandable," he answered, "but just try to pick it up from here."

"Okay," I said, making a mental note to just talk and not get lost in my thoughts.

I picked up the story where I had drifted off. "I screamed, but it was just a short outburst because he pulled his arm more tightly around me and covered my mouth and said, 'Callate.'"

I don't really speak Spanish, but I knew the word, and more than that, I knew by his movements he didn't want me to make any more noise. He started dragging me backwards across the deck, into my bedroom. Standing behind me, he was talking quickly in Spanish. He pulled my arms behind my back and started tying my hands together. I felt something warm running down my legs, soaking into my jeans. "How funny," I thought, "he's stabbed me and it didn't even hurt when he stuck the knife in." I bent my head down to look, expecting to see a pool of red at my feet. Instead, it was only clear, wet and clear. I couldn't remember ever being scared enough to wet my pants. And while my head was down, that's when he put another cloth over my eyes and tied it.

I slipped back into my thoughts and remembered how I had suddenly become more aware of what was happening, taking a bit of control and trying to figure out what to do. I decided it was like when I was a kid playing blind man's bluff. I knew if I kept my head down there would be a little bitty space, right there under my eyes, and I could cheat and still see. And then snapping back into the present I realized that wasn't the point. The point was, why is he tying me up?

I tried to think it through. I assumed he dragged me into the bedroom to rape me. But now he was tying me up. How would he get my clothes off if I'm all tied up? Oh, this is different ... strange. I had never been tied up before. If he's not going to rape me, what *is* he going to do?

I didn't have time to think about what his intentions were because he started dragging me backwards again, out of the room and back onto the deck. This time we turned to the left to walk off the back side of the deck, and I felt him reach down and pick something up. I remembered I had left a Mexican blanket there on the chair, and briefly wondered why he would want it. And then, half pushing me, half guiding me, we were down the small steps and out the back gate of the fence surrounding the house. He stopped suddenly and took the time to wrap the blanket around us both, making a single silhouette.

I knew we were leaving the house and walking into the desert. Another old memory surged up inside me as I thought about being a kid and going to the dentist. I always wanted to pull back, and yank on momma's hand and stumble, and trip, and beg, beg PLEASE don't make me go, mamma ... please ... please. I felt like I wanted to do that.

But this was not a trip to the dentist. I knew he was taking me to the arroyo. I'd been there a hundred times. You know, Billy Pat, the arroyo running southeast, to Evelyn's ranch? The one that gets deeper and deeper, and *real* deep by the time the smaller arroyo cuts into it? Looking at me with sad eyes, Billy Pat answered, "Yeah ... the one that's like a little canyon it's so deep."

Realizing where we were going, I began to panic. "He's taking me to the arroyo to kill me. He will kill me and leave me there, deep in the desert, where no one but the coyotes will find me. Noah will never know what happened to me, he'll grow up an orphan, thinking I abandoned him ..." My thoughts only heightened my panic, and I thought my heart would explode. Walking faster now, he pulled me through scrub brush and cactus, yanking on my arm and muttering in Spanish in an angry tone.

Taking a long pause in recounting all that had happened, I wondered if I should tell the assembled officials about the most unbelievable parts of the gruesome story. There were things that happened out in that desert that, yes, were horrible. Things so sad and scary that they really could "make a grown man cry". But there were other parts too. Strange and wonderful things that couldn't be explained by our present understanding. I debated with myself. "Should I tell them all of those parts too?" I thought. "Maybe they don't care about anything other than what he did, how he did it, and how many times," my cynical side reasoned. Too tired to think about it anymore, I decided to just blurt everything out.

"Now, you probably won't believe what I'm about to tell you," I said to all the people stuffed into the room, silently watching me and seeming to hang on every word I said. "Or maybe you will, if you've heard something like this before. Maybe I lost my mind and went a little crazy, I don't know. I have my own opinion on what it was, but I won't bother you with opinion, I'll just go on."

It was something so bizarre, so strange, so out-of-my-experience I couldn't explain it to myself and I couldn't quite understand what was happening while it was happening. A voice, calm and strong, and loud enough to fill my mind completely and block all of my panicked thoughts began speaking to me. With little effort, I listened intently to what the voice was saying.

"*Don't be afraid,*" the voice instructed me. "*You are not alone and your fear will only hurt you. Ignore your fear and listen to what I say. Do exactly what I tell you to do. Do not lie to this man. Don't give in to fear.*"

Now everyone in the examining room was silently staring straight at me. I couldn't read their expressions, but I assumed they thought I was crazy. I even thought I was crazy. Nevertheless, it was true. "And that's not the only time the voice spoke to me," I said, "but I'll tell you about that in a minute."

Time was passing and I assumed they wanted the facts ... "*Just the facts, Ma'm,*" as they say.

So now that I had revealed the crazy part, I was ready to go on telling them what had happened. It was the "crazy part" that was the miracle to me, and the part to try and figure out. I didn't know it then, but the question of what, or who, the voice was, would consume me for the rest of my life. And more than that, the quest to find the answer would change my life forever.

8

Physical vs Spiritual

WE GOT TO THE BARBED wire fence that crosses the arroyo and he told me to stop. The amazing thing was, he told me to stop in Spanish and I understood every word he said. I didn't have to try and guess what he was talking about, I understood him!

He began taking off the gag, and untied my hands. He was still behind me, and I hadn't had even a glimpse of him. Then he began to take off the blindfold. "Abra los ojos," he commanded.

"It's ok," I told him, "you don't have to take off the blindfold.

"Abra los ojos" he repeated in a stronger tone.

"No, it's okay. I'll walk better, I don't need to open my eyes. I haven't seen you, I don't know who you are. I'll never be able to identify you." I was bargaining with him to convince him I couldn't identify him. I wanted him to understand that he didn't have to kill me. Amazed at myself, I told him all of that *in Spanish*. I was speaking fluent Spanish.

He told me to be quiet. I kept my eyes shut. Because we were so far into the desert, and so deep into the arroyo, I knew we couldn't be seen from the highway. Not understanding why we were stopping and why he was untying me started to ignite the fear in the pit of my stomach. As my thoughts began to race, a wave of fear came crashing in on me, sucking at my legs like an undertow. The desert started to shift underneath me as I thought, "This is it. This is it. He'll stab me and the last thing I'll see is his monster face. He'll enjoy it, he'll be smiling ... smiling a sick, gruesome smile and breathing hard with every thrust of his knife."

He told me again to "open your eyes". This time I did. He stood a few feet across the arroyo from me, smiling a crooked grin. He had an odd expression on his face, a mixture of hate and fun.

Now I hesitated again, wondering if I should share what came next with the people in the room. "They aren't going to believe you anyway, and it will make you sound like some holy roller who's practiced this sort of thing her whole life. How am I going to explain the explosion of light? The utter calm? How it feels after a wave crashes over you and when you reach the top of the water the world is reflected in prism fragments, none of the pieces quite matching up with the other pieces?" But I quickly decided that what happened next should be shared with the folks recording the whole thing. It was so momentous, had such magnitude, I didn't think I would make sense if I didn't share it.

"You may not believe this," I started, "but this is exactly what happened next."

I opened my eyes and the light around me caught me by surprise. It seemed funny to me that after everything that had happened, I could still be surprised, but I was. The voice spoke to me again, and again in the calm, commanding tone, *"Forgive this man."*

I was staring at him now, disbelieving what I was hearing in my head. I started to argue with the voice. "FORGIVE HIM?" I screamed in my mind. "He's going to kill me! He's going to make my child an orphan!"

"Forgive this man," the voice intoned, never wavering.

"Why should I forgive him? He's a monster! I HATE him!" my mind screamed again.

Never changing tone or cadence, the voice again said, *"Forgive this man."*

Time stopped. Standing there looking at him was like looking through a prism in front of a flame. As if my mind had hands and fingers, I grasped and clawed to search for some rational explanation of what was happening. Reaching out with my arms, now, I watched as he slowly lowered the knife to his side. He was only about three feet away from me. His eyes, wide as plates, had a look of incredulity, almost fear. His complexion was white as alabaster.

"Pobrecito, Pobrecito. Lo siento mucho. I forgive you," I said, as I walked toward him and put my arms around him. I felt a thundering torrent of forgiveness wash over me, electrifying me. I held him like that for a minute, then I stepped back.

Finally, I remembered an experience I could liken it to. It was like a kid jumping off the high dive into the far below swimming pool. The silent stance and staring so far, far down into the deep blue water ... the moments sliding by, unnoticed, while you gathered your courage. When denial was no longer a possibility, the slow, endless fall through the hot summer air of nothing. The impact. The sudden weight of complete immersion. The loud crack of icy water catching you, holding you, cradling your weight all the way to the bottom.

You did it! You did it, and the joy and freedom burst inside along your needy lungs. You push, hard, with toes and calves and flexed knees and the rise to the top is straight and fast, and like an arrow you cut through your own wake. Your eyes are open and filled with the blue pool. Your head is thrown back and the blazing summer light fragments everything you see in sharp disjointed angles.

The light surrounding me now was like that. I had a translation I could understand. And now the voices and the visions seemed like one thing.

I looked straight at him for what seemed like a long time. His crazy, twisted smile was melting, fading into something sad and dark. As for me, I felt illuminated.

We stood like that, not moving, while the light and the voice and the desert gathered around us. Some feeling of unknowable resignation was washing over both of us, washing over the poor ragged children living in hell. For some reason I couldn't fathom, the forgiveness had been mine. Unable to give forgiveness, I had been given it. And after being drenched in its power, I was able to give it to him.

I felt as if I were standing in the midst of grandeur. I felt like no matter what happened next, it was going to be all right. The calm voice spoke and said if I could stand in this place it would be all right. It would be long, and terrible and strange, and it would break my heart, but if I could stand it, it would be all right.

His face suddenly changed again, as if returning to the self he knew. He threw the blanket on the ground and told me to take off my clothes. I did.

"And why isn't he getting undressed?" I wondered. The wave, the wave again is building. I can feel it rushing, faster and closer. I'm afraid. He's pushing me, pushing me down to my knees, and he's standing there, standing and unbuttoning his jeans. NO! I don't want to do this. He can't, he can't! Pushing my head into him and I can't believe it. But there's a sore, oozing and raw and he can't, he can't want me to do this. My mind was engulfed again in full fear. I visualized him holding the knife in both hands poised above my back. Sudden clarity forced its way into my thoughts.

"What difference does V.D. make? He's going to kill me."

Afterwards he asked me if I wanted a cigarette. I said I did, and we sat there on the ground smoking as the dark night closed in on us. It was almost like two normal people. He was calm, I was calm. His whole demeanor seemed to have changed. We had a short conversation and, while I was trying to figure out what was going to happen next, he seemed to be relaxing and almost proud of himself for his kindness in offering me a smoke.

He asked me if I had been afraid when he grabbed me. "Si," I said, "Tenía mucho miedo." I added, "Y tu? Tienes miedo?" I asked the question with an innocent look while, guilty, I broke off a twig from a nearby greasewood bush and stuffed it and the cigarette butt into my pocket.

"Me? Why should I be afraid?" he answered. "You're the one who's going to die."

9

And There's More

Too much to think about. Now he's telling me something and talking fast. I don't understand.

He jumped up and stared out over the arroyo as if he expected someone to be there. He began to curse, muttering something I could barely hear. He was looking at this watch and punctuating his garble with "Shit!" or "Fuck!" the only English words he seemed to know. I moved over to stand by him and my gazes followed his as he looked in every direction. "What's the matter?" I asked, "What's wrong?" The fear begins again. Another wave, building up from far away, even while I anticipate the full force of its crash.

"What? What do you mean? I don't understand." He's talking faster, meaner now. He draws his finger across his throat.

He told me to be quiet, to sit down and shut up. Again, he looked at his watch and muttered obscenities. I moved back to my side of the arroyo as he began pacing a small area and kicking the dirt. I could understand bits and pieces of what he said, and it was clear to me that he was waiting for someone. I asked again, quietly, who he was waiting for. "My friends," he said, "they should be here already. It is going to be too late."

I felt paralyzed. I could feel sweat on my forehead, and I tried to knock back the wave of fear that was building on the edge of my consciousness. My mind was beginning the jumble of thoughts, projections, what-ifs. I could taste the panic.

My mind racing, I started trying to figure out what he was talking about. "There are more of them ... five more he said? Why are they coming out here to meet him? Was this all arranged, planned to the minute? He will kill me and they will watch, but not until they have all ... what will they do to me? Five more, six, counting him again. I can't stand it, I WON'T stand it. It's going to hurt too much, I'll lose my mind ... and then they will kill me. A little bit at a time, cutting away small pieces, laughing, watching my pain. I won't be able to scream because ..."

"Stop it. You cannot do this. I told you not to indulge in your fear. What you think will happen. Don't think. Listen to me ... LISTEN! Empty your mind and listen."

The desert was quiet and still and he had turned around again to look out over the silver emptiness. Nothing moved. He turned around and squatted, his back against the arroyo wall. Directly opposite each other now, his eyes bored into me in silent ... was it hatred? No. It was more like inconvenience. He was sulking.

"Why do we need your friends?" I asked softly. "Maybe they're lost, maybe they're not coming."

"They have all my things. They were supposed to bring them to me. Now it is too late."

"Too late for what?" I asked in the same low voice.

"You see the moon? The stars? It's a long way to Lajitas, and I'll never get there before light!" and he cursed again, words I didn't understand.

Like some sort of magic suspended animation my fear stopped. It hung somewhere in mid-air and the voice began again.

"Very good, I told you all you have to do is listen. He needs his friends. Be one. Here are your choices: he needs money, he needs to get to the river before daylight. Tell him."

"Getting to the river is no problem," I almost whispered. His eyes darted to the knife by his leg as he watched me get up and move to his side of the arroyo. I stood close by him and looked out over the desert, my arms resting on the top of the arroyo. "Didn't you see my truck?" I asked, "I can take you to Lajitas in about 20 minutes."

He stood up, looking a little confused and I could see he was trying to think of a new plan.

"It is not easy for him to think. You can see how one thought takes a long time to connect to the next one. Go slow, and pretend you are thinking yourself. Give him many things to think about."

"I have money at my house," I started. He sneered and seemed annoyed. "Not anymore. I took your money."

Caught off-guard, I stared at him wide-eyed. "You took my money? All of it?" I blurted out.

"Well, just what was in your bag," he said hesitantly, looking like a scolded child.

"Take your time. Convince him there is more money. You need to return to your house. Tell him you have more ... and you do. You have checks and credit cards. You can explain those to him later."

"Did you look, um, over the ah, how do you say it? The chingadera, the thing arriba the ... Oh I don't know how to say it," I lied.

"Over the WHAT! What are you saying?" he barked.

"I don't know how to tell you, I don't know the right words! But I have money at my house, a lot of money. I'll give it to you. It's hidden, you couldn't have found it. I'll give it to you and then I can drive you to the river," I said again, mixing in the Spanish words I knew with the English words he didn't.

I waited for the possibilities to sink in. He was staring at me again, looking for traces of lies.

"You see, he gets nervous when the has many things to think about."

He looked at his watch again, then at the sky. He stared for a long time into the desert. Finally, he started talking, telling me what he would do. "You see that mountain over there? We are going there."

"But my house is the other way," I argued, "we don't need to go to that mountain."

"Shut up!" he yelled, suddenly angry again. "I need to get my friends and my things. I will tie you up and gag you and put the rag over your eyes. I will only be gone a little while. You will wait on the mountain."

"But what about the money, and the truck? I thought we would go ..."

"SHUT UP!" he yelled again, as he dropped the poncho and tried to hold on to the knife.

"What, what do you mean? I don't understand," I said softly, trying not to make him any angrier than he already was.

He drew his finger across his throat and then placed one finger in front of his lips, daring me to say another word. He told me to pick up the blanket and hand it to him. I did what he asked and as soon as he touched it, he dropped the blanket again and slapped my face in one easy movement. It was so fast and so violent, and I was caught off balance as I was moving toward him.

It almost felt good to be stunned. I couldn't think. I was limp and felt a moment of the sagging weight of this ordeal. "How long has it been?" I wondered, feeling so tired I could just lay here on the ground and let him do whatever he wanted.

"You will not cry and you are not tired. There is no time to be tired. You will get up and wait. You will not speak."

I slowly wrapped my fingers around the poncho and stood up, keeping my eyes fixed on the ground. He stood inches away, holding the knife.

He grabbed a corner of the fabric and together we held the blanket while he took the knife and began to cut the poncho into strips. He began to slice downward, through the loosely woven fabric. The blade touched my belly and he held it there staring into my face. Without thinking I sucked in my stomach, and a slow smile crossed his face. He made another sawing motion with the knife, this time just nicking my skin. I looked at the tiny red line beginning to show on my belly and then into his eyes. "Here, let me help you," I said softly as I pulled the sides of the poncho tighter. Our eyes were locked onto each other as we stood that way, unmoving. Something shifted and without a word he began to cut the poncho into strips. I know the strips are for me, and I am helping him. There is something so strange hidden behind the slanted black buttons that are his eyes. There is something strange there and I want to know what it is.

"Put on your shirt," he said, "and let's go. Don't make even a single sound." He stuffed the strips of the poncho into his back pocket and with the knife in the other hand, climbed out over the arroyo. He reached down with one hand and grabbed my wrist. "Andele," he said and pulled me up out of the arroyo.

10

The Mountain

HE KEPT HOLDING MY HAND after he had pulled me out of the arroyo. "How odd," I kept thinking, "It's like I'm his girlfriend or something and we're just going for a moonlight walk. This is crazy. He must be crazy." I wondered if he had ever had a girlfriend. I wondered if he treated all women the way he had treated me, as an object, something only to satisfy his wants, regardless of the pain he inflicted. I wondered if he enjoyed their pain. Walking through the desert in silence, these thoughts filled my mind. It was better than thinking of what might happen once we reached the mountain. It was better than being afraid of what might happen next.

We trudged on and on and threaded our way between cactus, rocks and greasewood. The mountain looked so far away, but the closer we got to it, the bigger it was.

Time didn't seem to be a factor for me anymore. With every step I felt a little closer to my death. "Why the mountain?" I couldn't stop wondering. "What reason could he be taking me there except to kill me?" I thought. "At least somebody will see my body up on that mountain," I reasoned. "They'll use helicopters and small planes to look for me, the way they try to find hikers who get lost out here every year. But what about that boy they never found? Is his body on top of a mountain, blended into the rocks and cactus, torn to pieces by predators, still waiting?" I asked myself.

"Do not talk to yourself this way. Nothing is happening. You are walking in the desert. A man is holding your hand. Do not convince yourself to be afraid. You are only walking in the desert now."

Every time the voice spoke to me it took me by surprise. So many things to think about. Was this me talking to me? Why was the voice so calm? Why was the voice always so right?

I began to try to make small conversation with him, as much to hear my own voice, if I still had one, as to convince him of anything. "Let's don't walk so fast," I tried, "I can hardly keep up with you."

"Quiet. Don't talk. Just walk," he said.

To take my attention off of where we were going, I studied the way the moon lighted the desert. What is white by day becomes silver under a full moon. What is green, becomes black. Everything seemed extra-real. And like looking into stereoscopic lenses, everything jumps out at you in three dimensions.

He stopped. We were at the base of the mountain. He squatted down and pulled me with him. I watched as he looked in all directions. "Like some kind of animal," I thought. "His eyes show suspicion like an animal."

We walked a little more to the west, and before us was an incline of steep loose gravel. He pulled on my arm to motion that this was the way we would go. "Great," I thought, "they'll never see tracks on this rock." He pulled on my arm again, and I took the first step up the eerie incline.

Rocks would slip now and then, and the sound was hollow as they tumbled down the slope. I was getting a bad feeling again.

47

Another wave was building just out of my consciousness. A part of me knew it was there and another part of me tried to beat down its rising swell. It was harder going now; the climb was getting steeper. Or was I getting tired? "No, I can't be tired," I cautioned myself. "There's too much left to do. I'm a long way from home. I have to get myself back home." I was sweating, even in the cool night desert, I was sweating.

I could see the top now. Just a little bit further. He quickened the pace and I fell in step with him, eager in a horrible way, to get to the top. We had reached a flat place, almost like a mesa, about fifty yards from the top. Off to the west was a bit more of an incline, and it looked as if it was all some sort of loose stone. I looked to the east and across the miles, saw the school, so tiny in the distance. I looked south and saw my friend Evelyn's ranch. It looked almost close enough to run to. I could hear her dogs barking in the distance.

He stopped and told me to sit down. He squatted beside me and offered me a cigarette. While we smoked, he started talking to me, quietly, almost in a whisper. The effect of the tone of his voice was like a stab through my heart. I was wrapped in fear. "I am going to tie you up," he said as he pulled the strips of the poncho out of his pocket and neatly laid them across his knee. "I am going to put the rags around your eyes, tie your feet together and your hands together. There is no need to put the rag in your mouth."

Without thinking I began to try to talk to him. "You don't need to tie me up! I can go with you! Or I can wait here for you, I won't ..."

"Be quiet," he said. "I am going to tie you up and leave you here, only for a little while. I have to go to the other side of this mountain and get my things. There is a little hut there, where I live. My things are there."

I began to beg. "Please don't leave me here! I can go with you! I'm not tired!"

"You can't go with me!" he snapped, and I could tell he was getting angry again. "I am going to tie you up and leave you here! If you try to get away, I will hear you and I will come back and kill you. I can watch you from where I am going. If you make a sound or try to get away, I will kill you and they will never find you!"

He began to tie my ankles together. Still begging, I was using any excuse to try to get him to leave me untied. "If you leave me here tied up the coyotes will eat me! What if a rattlesnake is here? You can't leave me tied up out here! I'm afraid, I'm afraid ..."

Now he was tying my hands together. "Shut up. These are stupid things to be afraid of," he spat at me. "If you make any more noise, I will tie your mouth, too, or I will just kill you now!"

I didn't say anything else as I watched him move stones and rocks to make some kind of indention in the loose gravel. "He is going to kill me. Why else would he just leave me here?" My thoughts going wild, near panic. Now he was digging with one of the flat stones, hollowing out a niche. "It's my grave he's digging," I thought, "A shallow grave that he'll cover with the stones he placed to the side. No wonder he doesn't want to gag me. I won't be making any noise."

I sat silently and considered the situation. My ploy about the money at the house hadn't worked. He was just worried about getting to Lajitas before dawn. Maybe he already had the keys to my truck and would just drive himself. "It doesn't matter," I thought as an empty, silent, and strangely restful feeling overtook me. "I won't know how this all ends. My body won't be found and my son will spend his life wondering what happened to the only family he ever had. My son. I wish there was some way for him to know how much I love him. I hope he learns that love is all there is. My son ..."

He was through digging now. The shallow indentation was just a couple of feet away, and he motioned for me to slide over into it. He watched my face, saw the tears beginning to well in my eyes. He bent down and helped move me into the small crevice. He was behind me, his breath warm on my neck. "I am going to cover your eyes now," he began in a tight quiet voice. "Don't try to untie yourself. You'll never make it to that ranch down there. If you try, I will kill you when I catch you. Don't make a sound. I will only be gone just a little while."

A small thread of hope began to cut through the rising swell of fear. "Maybe he won't kill me. Maybe he'll do what he says. Oh God, don't let him stab me to death on this mountain," I cried silently. My eyes were covered now, and I felt small and totally alone.

"Remember what I said. I'll be watching you," he whispered, "Or I will come back and kill you." I could hear his footsteps and the loose gravel giving way under them. I could hear so clearly. I knew he was going up the gravelly slope, and could tell how far away he was, when suddenly his footsteps stopped. I knew he was at the top of the slope and I could sense him crouching there, watching me. I sat absolutely motionless. I heard a few more footsteps and then he was gone.

Where was my voice, my director, now? I tried to call it back by going over my choices, one by one. If I could untie myself, I might make it to the ranch below. If I could only get close to the ranch, Evelyn's dogs would set up a howl. But what if I didn't get close enough? What if the dogs were inside? What if Evelyn was in town? What if, what if ... my thoughts droned on. I could try to run for my house. But I was further away from it than he was. What if he caught me midway? He would kill me, take my truck, and leave for Mexico.

The voice still wasn't talking. The air was gentle, the night growing cooler every hour. What would he do with me when he came back? Probably take me to my house, get the money, and have me drive him to the river. Nothing made any sense. Any one of the choices was just as good as another. Tears rolled out of my eyes, unbidden, and I heard myself begin to pray.

"Our Father, who art in heaven, hallowed be Thy name. Thy kingdom come Thy will be done, on earth as it is in heaven." The rest of it didn't matter, and I slipped right into, *"And yea, though I walk through the valley of the shadow of death, I will fear no evil, for Thou are with me. Thy rod and Thy staff they comfort me. Surely goodness and mercy ..."* I was sobbing now, my shoulders bent and shaking. There was no way out. I was going to die, now or in a little while. And death? It was a shadow. I could see that now. The words repeated by themselves, over and over in my head. I watched myself become curiously calm. The tears were not of fear. In fact, they felt like a kind of cleansing. There were no more thoughts of what might happen, no dwelling on what had already happened. "How odd" I thought. "I always believed when you died, you died completely alone. Now I know that you don't. That presence is always with you. You're never alone."

I was enveloped in peace.

11

Hansel and Gretel

AT FIRST IT WAS JUST one loose stone, bouncing down the incline. I caught my breath, stretching my senses to hear more sound. Then a couple of fast steps. My heartbeat was pounding in the still night, just as a cavalcade of rocks and gravel started to shift.

"He's coming back! I can't believe he's coming back!" I thought with a stunned disbelief. I had secretly hoped he would decide to just leave me there and go on with his friends to Lajitas, or forget the whole nightmare and pretend it had never happened. Now it was evident the night was far from over.

"I don't want any more of this!" my thoughts screamed. "I can't take this, I want this to stop! I can't ..." my thoughts flew into a thousand directions. I felt like a million "Me"s all thinking at the same time, and all the thoughts at the extreme end of whatever emotion they were expressing. There was even a "Me" that calmly watched the chaotic dissolution of myself.

Then I heard the slide of gravel and his cursing. The last rock tumbled to a standstill, and his words were rough and mean. Then he was walking toward me and I could sense his mood was ugly.

"I fell on the fucking rocks! Goddamn pricks. GET UP!" he yelled.

I tried to stand but with my ankles tied and no hands to help it was impossible. I ended up only wriggling in the dirt, and then suddenly he was beside me.

"So, the fucking coyotes and vipers didn't eat you, huh! Goddamn bitch," he muttered. He untied my ankles and reached for the blindfold, ripping it off my eyes and leaving it around my neck. His face was sweaty and his lip curled tightly around his bottom teeth. He got up and walked behind me and yanked me to my feet by my still tied hands. Once I was standing, he untied my hands and I saw a small but new pack on the ground next to him. He picked it up and slung it over one shoulder. He still held the poncho strips in one hand, and grabbed my arm with the other one.

Without another word we started walking down the mountain the same way we had come up. To the right of me was a steep drop-off, and he threw one of the strips he had tied me with into the abyss. A few more steps and another tie was thrown. It reminded me of Hansel and Gretel and the trail of crumbs they left so they could find their way back home. "This trail of rags," I thought, "will be proof of what he has done, and will mark my way back home. Home. "We're going home!" I thought with more relief coursing through my body than I had ever known. It was a feeling of sheer joy. I felt light, and happy, as if I could fly off the mountain. "I'm alive! We're going back to my house!" I couldn't contain my thoughts and I wondered if I was smiling. I watched silently, bursting with a kind of total freedom as he threw away the last tie. He couldn't tie me up anymore ... I was free.

As we came to the bottom of the mountain he stopped. He told me to sit on the ground and I did as I was told, feeling uneasy about why we were stopping so soon on our trip back to the house. He stood above me, leering with a kind of focused stare. He unzipped his pants and told me to take off my jeans. My thoughts were thrown immediately back into fear, and the dichotomy between my joy of just moments ago and the sudden recognition of what he was about to do made my thoughts unintelligible. I literally felt torn into pieces, like I was a hundred different "Me"s. And none of the pieces connected with any of the other ones. I started to cry as he climbed on top of me. For one clear moment my thoughts told me to scratch the ground so that dirt would be under my fingernails. Lying on my back, scratching the earth, and gazing through my tearful eyes, I stared at the stars. I tried to become one with the heavens so I wouldn't know what was happening down here in hell. "*Just do what he says,*" the voice said softly. "*It is of no importance. You are going home.*"

He finished and stood up, then told me to put my jeans on. Looking west, toward the highway several hundred yards away, he grabbed my hand and said only, "Come." We walked northwest, toward my house and parallel to the highway. In a daze I still felt like I had won the war. We'd go home, I'd get my truck and drive him to the border. The voice was going to protect me. The voice promised I would be okay.

Then my thoughts began to slow as I remembered I'd promised to give him money. I knew I didn't have any. "Maybe he'll forget about that," I thought, and then felt supremely foolish. "Yeah, right, he's going to forget all about the big money you promised him. He's just a regular fella out having a good time on a Saturday night." My sense of freedom was evaporating. His mood was so dark and ugly I could only imagine how he'd take the news.

Whatever was going to happen, I couldn't think about it now. "At least I'll be home," I thought, "where everything will be familiar. If he kills me, at least it won't be out in the desert."

We came to a barbed wire fence and he crouched down, pulling me with him. He looked up and down the fence line and seemed confused. "Shit!" he muttered. I was trying to read his thoughts, watching him for any clues. "Fuck! We're in the wrong place!" he rasped, saving me the energy of second guessing him.

"It's okay," I started, "we can see the house from here."

He yanked my arm, hard, and I lost my balance, falling over onto one leg. "You talk so fucking much, you bitch! Don't say anything more to me until I tell you to talk!" He stood up slightly, and still crouching we edged along the fence line, going west now. I could still see the highway. We both saw the lights of a passing car at the same time. He pushed me to the ground and flattened himself beside me. He was muttering to himself so fast I couldn't understand the words. But I knew he was mad. We lay there for a minute while I tried to catch some phrase I would know. The car passed and he said, "We're too close to the road. We have to go back."

I couldn't believe it. Go back! Exhaustion settled over me like sifting dust. I was thirsty. I was tired, more tired than I'd ever been in my life. I could see my house, just a few hundred yards and we'd be there. I was so tired I didn't know if I could even move. "Go back," I thought. "We're not going to the house, I'll never see my house again, he's just playing with me. I can't finish this," I thought, feeling all energy drain out of me, like a balloon, losing all its air.

"These thoughts won't help you," the voice interrupted. *"I have reminded you to stay present, and I remind you again. If you are tired you will go on. 'Tired' has nothing to do with it. I am still with you."*

And now I had to think about the voice, and him, and me all at the same time. I was breaking up again, starting to watch myself multiply, by division. In some sort of attempt to find sense of everything in why this was happening, I whispered to him in a small voice, "Why me? Why did you stop at my house? Why not some other house? What made you pick me?" The sound of my voice brought me back to a sense of wakefulness.

"Perros," he said. "You don't have any dogs," he said simply. "Let's go."

We started walking back down the fence line, heading east, away from the highway and away from my house. Away from my last hope of help. There were more cars now on the highway, more headlights. "Everyone's coming home from the dance," I thought. A quick calculation told me it was probably around 1:30 or 2:00. "How odd," I wondered. "Everything is still normal for all those people. They had a good time, danced, drank, joked with each other, argued over petty differences. I'm dying and the world can go on like nothing has happened. To them, nothing has happened." I felt a deep sadness, a loss like no other. Maybe nothing in the world connected after all. We were all just so many lone stragglers, living our own stories.

He stopped and, dragging along behind him, I bumped into him. I was absorbed in my thinking. I looked north and could see my house. We were well to the east of it. I looked at the fence line. We were right back where we'd started, where he had taken off the blindfold and untied my hands. He slipped under the fence via the hollowed-out space we had crawled through earlier. He lifted the bottom wire and motioned for me to follow him. We weren't going back to the arroyo. We were going home.

12

The House

WE WALKED WITHOUT SPEAKING TO within a hundred yards of my back fence. I was surprised to see all the lights were on in the house. Evidently, I had turned on lights before I had walked to the patio to see the moon rise, before all of this had started. Of course, neither one of us had thought to turn lights off.

He stopped and looked at me, his eyes dark sockets of evil. "If anyone comes to your house, you're dead right here," he rasped. We stood there for maybe 5 minutes, watching the few random cars coming from the dance pass by. Lights blazing in the house at 2:00 in the morning was a perfect invitation for any of my friends to stop, a signal that the party could continue at my house. I prayed. Even as I tried to convince him that no one would stop at this time of morning, my thoughts were screaming to the passing cars to go on home. And of course, there was the observer in me, commenting on how ironic it was to be in such circumstances and still bid the passing cars to pass me by.

Finally, he was ready to walk up to the house. He put his arm around my shoulders and stuck the knife to my throat. "You better hope no one is home," he whispered. "Let's go." We walked through the gate and up to the patio. The front door was standing open, just as I had left it.

"Do you have any guns?" he asked as he jerked me closer into him and tightened his grip on the knife.

"No," I said. "I don't have any guns. I don't even know how to use a gun!"

We walked through the front door and he kicked it closed behind us. "Now where is the money?" he growled. I walked over to my handbag, opened it and brought out my wallet. Empty. I wheeled around, surprising him. "It's gone! My money is gone!" I shouted. I knew I had put about $50 in the wallet before I left town, and for it to be gone meant someone had stopped by the house while I was in the desert, or, maybe I had lost it, or ... his eyes were wide and he shrugged when the thought finally hit me. "Did you, did you take it?" I asked as the words dropped in front of me and I slowly realized he must have been inside the house before he grabbed me while I was standing outside. How long had he been there? Had it been a cat and mouse game as he waited for darkness? No wonder I had felt so uneasy. No wonder my thoughts kept urging me to leave the house. Were those thoughts MY thoughts, or an early version of the voice?

His face began to harden as he realized our roles were reversed. I was asking the questions, accusing him, even shouting at him. He walked across the room towards me, slowly, his eyes set in a hard, grim gaze. Pushing me into the wall, hard, he said, "And where is the money 'arriba'? You said you had money hidden. Where is it?"

"I, I didn't know the word for it, I meant the money in my bag," I lied. "This was the money I meant to give you. Now it's gone," and I cast my eyes downward and pretended I didn't know he had already stolen it. "But it doesn't matter!" I began. "I have checks, and credit cards, and I'll give them to you! Look! See, you can take them and I'll show you how ..." with that I pushed away from the wall and grabbed my handbook. I spread the checks and credit cards in front of him on the dining room table. I patiently showed him the balance in my checkbook. "How much do you want the checks to be for?" I asked, tearing a couple from the book and signing my name. He told me to make one for $300 and the other one for $250.

"But, how will I cash them?" he asked, a little confused.

"That's no problem," I said, sounding like his best friend. "Just take this VISA card for identification. You can also take the card to any bank and get up to $1,000 cash."

He stood looking at the checks and the visa card with a blank stare. I could still hear a passing car now and then, and I was still praying no one would stop. I walked over to my handbag and got the keys to my truck. I was anxious to get him to the border, and feeling more secure now that I was in my own house and handing out money like I was "Miss Big Bucks". He walked over to his back pack and put the checks and visa card into a side pocket.

He looked up at me then, and his eyes were ungrateful, uncaring, dead. Picking up the knife, he stood and grabbed my arm, then turned me around and started pushing me toward the bathroom. The room was long and narrow, incorporating a dressing room with the shower at the other end. "I want to take a shower," he said softly, "you, too."

I didn't understand. I was so sure this night would be over once I made it back to the house. So sure. "This means," my thoughts began, "this means he's not leaving, there's more, more to get through, more ..."

And in the next instant he shoved me toward the shower and yelled, "Fix the fucking water!" His anger kept my thoughts hanging in the air, unfinished.

"Take off your clothes and get in," he ordered, and I did. The water was hot and soothing to my aching body. I felt filthy. He had his clothes off, now, and stepped in. The minute the water touched him he made a sort of yelp, and pulled his hand back, ready to slap me. Then he noticed I was just standing under the water, it wasn't too hot for me. A short look of lost manliness crossed his face, and I quickly acted. "I'm sorry! I didn't think it was that hot! Do you want it to be cooler?" I asked, trying to sound like I cared.

"No, no," he said, and instead of slapping me, moved me to one side while he stepped under the steamy water. I handed him the soap and he handed it back to me. "You do it," he said, and a slow sickening smile started at the sides of his mouth.

"I can't take it," I thought, and I could feel the tears mixing with the water on my face. "This has to stop, it's worse than a nightmare, it won't stop, it won't stop!"

He was in control again, and it looked like he intended to enjoy it. He put his hands on my shoulders and pushed me down. Then something broke inside of me, and I was sobbing, shaking in the thick steam. He leaned against the shower wall and said simply, "Hurry up."

13

I Need a Hero

HE LEFT ME LIKE THAT, kneeling in the shower, while he dried off and got dressed. He reached in and turned off the water, and I pulled myself up holding onto the shower wall. I was lost in humiliation and disgust, not wanting to move, or think, or even breathe. I didn't feel human. Total degradation takes away more than your strength, it sucks everything you are out of your very soul, leaving you vacant, open. You are not anyone or anything. You are not.

He opened the door to the closet and stared at the underwear lined up on a shelf. He moved them around with the tip of the knife and said, "Pick out something pretty."

I put on a pair of pink underwear and a bra, and I was reaching for a T-shirt when he said, "That's enough." He turned me around and placed the tip of the knife to my back and, turning out the light, we started walking to the front door. To reach my bedroom we had to walk onto the patio, then down a stone walkway to the deck, then into my room. As we passed the spot where he had first grabbed me, I stopped, wondering how long ago it had been. It seemed like years. He pushed me onto the deck and into my bedroom, and the smell of that first fear still hung in the air.

The first thing he saw was the .22 rifle hanging on the wall. He threw me against the opposite wall and started screaming at me as he grabbed it. "You told me you didn't have a gun! You lying bitch, I'm going to kill you!" he screamed. I turned around and he was pointing the rifle at me. I froze.

"You must change his mind again. What have you learned? Think clearly and empty yourself of fear. What have you learned?"

The sound of the clear, patient voice made me realize I was watching everything from outside myself again. I was actually talking to him, telling him I didn't know it was there, that it wasn't mine, that a friend must have left it. I heard him screaming at me from some faraway place, but the words finally got through to me when he cut himself off in mid-sentence and said very quietly, "Put some music on the stereo." I was standing in front of the shelf that held the stereo, with cassette tapes stacked to the side. Time stopped, and the million "Me"s were all clamoring and sending out different messages, and still the voice spoke on, while at the same time I was thinking, "What music do you want to die to?"

"You are not ready to die. I told you from the beginning this would be the hardest thing you would ever do. Don't give up now, there is only a little more to go through. It is up to you to change his mind."

I picked out my favorite tape, *Apocalypse of the Animals*, and put it into the stereo. I turned around to face him, totally composed. He was standing there pointing the gun straight at me and I heard myself casually ask, "Are there bullets in it?"

He looked down at the gun, then held it out from himself like he was trying to see if it was loaded. I walked the few steps over to him and said, "How many bullets are in there?" He pulled back a piece of the gun and started shaking the bullets out onto the bed. I counted them for him. He pulled another lever on the gun and a long steel rod came loose. He pulled it out of the gun. In minutes, there were pieces of gun all over the bed.

The music was playing softly now, and to me both of us seemed suspended in some sort of slow motion. He began trying to put the rifle back together. He couldn't even get the bullets loaded. Finally, in disgust he threw it against the wall behind him, cursing.

"Get that goddamned music off!" he yelled. "Don't you have any dance music? Something fast!"

I put another tape in the cassette, Bonnie Tyler, *I Need a Hero*, almost smiling at the irony. He pushed me onto the bed and put the knife on the headboard. I lay there watching him take off his clothes, not really even caring what was about to happen, again. I was trying to figure out why and how everything changed every time I heard "the voice." It was so much more than coincidence. It wasn't my voice. It had been with me all night. I couldn't help imagining that maybe I was already dead and the voice was God, taking me through what would have happened if I had not died. I was totally disconnected now from what was actually happening, lost in the thoughts and comfort of the voice. He was on top of me, moving into me with a hard violence. I didn't feel it. I didn't move. I only thought about the voice.

He pulled away from me, grabbing my hands and holding them above my head. I wasn't really paying any attention, it was just another sudden, violent move. He slapped me, realizing I wasn't really even there, and wanting me to know and feel fear and pain. Or maybe he knew I was in shock and just wanted me to know what he was doing. The sting of the slap brought me back to the room and the present moment and the sick, cruel look in his eyes. "Roll over," he said.

There is no way to anticipate what you have never experienced, never even thought about. I simply did as he said without thinking about it. He bore into me with a suddenness and a violence I never expected. The pain ripped away my thoughts and left me screaming.

Amazingly, he stopped. I was sobbing, my face buried into a pillow. He bent forward and whispered into my ear, "Wait for a minute."

He got up and walked to his pack. I turned my head to look at him and saw him retrieve a large jar of some kind of pink cream. He began smearing it all over himself, watching me with a half grin. Now I could anticipate. Now I knew what he was going to do. He climbed back onto the bed behind me and bent toward my ear. "I have sisters," he whispered.

After he finished, we lay there on the bed while he smoked another cigarette, this time not offering one to me. I glanced at the knife laying on the headboard above us. For just a brief instant I thought that maybe I could grab it and either kill him or myself. At this point I wanted to die and it didn't seem to matter whether he did it or I did.

"Go ahead," he said quietly with an amused grin starting to spread over his mouth. "You won't make it."

"I wasn't going to try," I said softly.

14

Getting Out

WHEN HE HAD FINISHED HIS cigarette, he sat up and said, "Get up. I'm hungry." He got dressed, picked up the knife, and marched me, naked, back into the main house. "Now what," I thought. Surely, it's getting close to morning. Surely it will be light soon. I had no idea of what time it might be.

Once inside the house, he pointed me to the dressing room and said to get dressed. He stood in the doorway watching me while I picked out a pair of jeans and a T-shirt. My head was beginning to clear a little and I thought about the trip to the border in my truck. "What shoes do I want to have on if I have to walk through the desert again," I wondered. I reached for the cowboy boots I had been wearing when he brought the flat side of the knife down across my hands.

"No," he said, "not those. These," and he pointed to a pair of flip flops. I felt uneasy but didn't have time to think it through because he immediately said, "Now go fix some food ... quick."

He walked through the kitchen and over to the dining room table and sat down, facing me. I looked around the kitchen trying to think of what to fix. Trying to think if I could poison him with

65

something. Trying to think if I should get a knife for myself. He never took his eyes off me.

I saw the coffee pot and put it on the stove. Still half full of coffee from two days before, I started to heat it, thinking, "I hope he chokes on it." Going to the fridge, I found some lunchmeat and bread. Placing it on the counter, along with a jar of mustard, I made a sandwich for him. Taking the hot coffee and the sandwich to him, I sat down across from him. "You're not hungry?" he asked between bites.

I answered simply, "No."

"You are acting perfectly right. Just a little more and you will be free. Do not drive him south to the border. Go north. Tell him about your office and the money there. Convince him. Drive north."

I started talking to him in a matter of fact voice. "If you want more money, in cash, we can go to my office ... the post office," I started, watching to see if I had stirred any interest. "I have a lot of money there, and money orders, too. We could go there before I take you to the river."

Knowing that if I drove north I would find the EMS office within a mile, and the EMT and his girlfriend lived there. I was taking a chance that he would let me drive north for the lure of more money. I was taking a risk that he didn't know we would drive past the post office on the way to the EMS station. And even if he did recognize the EMS station and wouldn't let me turn in to the driveway, there was a small restaurant another couple of miles past that. The owner, Jim, lived on the premises in a small travel trailer. Just getting closer to where people were seemed to offer a way that I could escape.

To the south was only 17 miles of nothing but desolate country.

"Do not lie to this man," the voice suddenly said, and then repeated, *"Do not lie to this man."*

I recognized a desperation in my mind. I HAD to get out of this house and find some people ... anyone. I felt that time was running out, that I had no more time to hesitate and nothing to lose. I had to get out of my house and into my truck.

I told him again about the money at my office. I told him there were hundreds of dollars, and even more in money orders.

Finished eating now, he got up and said, "Andele." Picking up the knife he jerked his head toward the front door, motioning me to leave ahead of him. He grabbed my truck keys and started out the door and down the flagstone walk to the driveway.

I was elated! I was going to my truck! "I'm leaving and I'll find help! If not, I'll drive him to the river and send him on his way back to Mexico," I thought in a flurry of excitement. "This nightmare is going to be over," I thought, "and I managed to survive."

We reached the truck and I went to the driver's side first. He walked around to the passenger side and stood at the door for a moment, looking at me. "What is he waiting for?" I wondered. I opened my door and slid behind the wheel, closing the door softly. Finally, he opened the passenger door and slid into the front seat sideways, in an awkward motion. With his eyes trained on mine I saw a movement with his right arm out of the periphery of my vision. He slid the knife under his leg, all the while trying to hold my gaze so I wouldn't notice. Without taking my eyes off his, I wondered why he would try to hide the knife. "He's had the damn thing all night, threatening me with it. Why hide it now? What is he doing?" I silently asked myself.

With sudden and shocking understanding, I realized he was planning to kill me on the way to the border. "That's why he wanted me to wear flip flops instead of boots," I remembered. "He's been planning to kill me all along, between my house and Lajitas, in the totally desolate stretch of desert. He didn't want to alert me so he hid the knife, even after brandishing it all night. He is going to kill me after all."

Looking almost sheepish, he handed me the keys. I started the truck, drove to the end of the driveway, and hesitated for just a moment. "If I turn south toward Lajitas and the river I will have 17 miles of nothingness," I thought. "If I turn north towards Study Butte, the medics, and Poncho's restaurant, at least I have a chance of finding someone to help me." I had to at least try, one last time, to stay alive.

I turned north and started talking to him at the same time, hoping to keep him occupied and unaware that we were going the wrong way. "We'll stop at my office and get the rest of the money," I said, "but we'll have to make it look like we broke in. We can break the lock on the drawer where the money is kept and no one will know it was you. It will just be someone who broke into the post office." I was talking fast hoping he wouldn't notice we had just passed the post office. The next turn to the right was the medics. With a broad circle in front of their office there was plenty of room to pull in, and I thought about crashing into the building and stunning him long enough for me to get out of the truck and get John, the resident medic, out of bed.

As soon as I made the turn, he started screaming at me. "Turn around! Turn around! Esta no es la oficina postal! Aqui están los medicos!"

Trying to convince him otherwise, I was yelling as loud as he was. "Si Si! Son los dos! Medicos y oficina postal!" He wasn't buying it and I turned the wheel sharply to the right, heading back out onto the highway. Turning north again, I had one last chance.

He was upset and still yelling at me, talking so fast I couldn't understand him. I was trying to keep him busy, asking him if he wanted the money at the post office or not, my voice as loud as his, all the while heading the short distance to Poncho's Restaurant and the owner's house. With all the yelling and all the questions I kept asking, I could see he was confused, not sure of the decisions he should be making. Just as we approached Poncho's he noticed we were headed north, not south toward the border.

Almost hysterical now, he screamed, "Turn around! Turn around NOW!"

I made a left turn into the front drive of the restaurant, and at the same time noticed the two gasoline pumps installed in front. He was still yelling, as I made a split decision and rammed the accelerator into the floor of the truck. Clawing at the truck's door trying to get out, I turned my head to see him. The last thing I saw was him lunging at me with the knife in one hand and trying to grab the steering wheel with the other. My door swung wide. I jumped out of the truck, knees buckling and my ankles fighting the rocks and gravel of the driveway. "You're not going down," my mind screamed, "not after all this! RUN! RUN!"

My legs straightened out and I ran for the small trailer Jim lived in beside the restaurant. I cleared the small hedge in front of his sliding front door, ripped off the screen door and threw it over my shoulder. Grabbing the sliding door, I pulled it hard to the left, breaking the small lock that kept it closed, all the while screaming, "JIM! JIM! GET YOUR GUN! GET YOUR GUN!"

Still half asleep, Jim came walking into the room. All I could do was continue to yell at him to "Get your gun!" With a confused look on his face he finally said, "All right, all right," and turned to go back into his bedroom to retrieve his gun. I don't know what happened next. I couldn't hear, and I couldn't speak. I couldn't even see. The next thing I knew, we were standing outside the deputy Sheriff's house and he was asking me what was wrong. I found out later that my mouth was moving as I tried to tell him, but no sound was coming out. And I couldn't understand why he kept asking me the same question over and over. "What is wrong?"

15

New Beginnings

"I GUESS YOU GUYS KNOW whatever happened after that," I said, hopefully finishing the story we were all crowded in the small room to hear. I was praying they wouldn't ask any questions, and praying I could now find a place to go to sleep.

"Just a couple of questions now, if that's all right," the deputy said quietly. I nodded my acceptance, and he went on. "Were you held against your will?"

"Yes."

"Were you sexually assaulted?"

"Yes."

"Were you in fear for your life?"

"Yes." The room was quiet as a tomb.

The deputy and the constable then both stood up and thanked me and said they would be in touch. The woman from the crises center told me she would have some clothes for me by the time I was ready to leave the hospital. A nurse walked me to the end of the hall to a small room. Exhausted, all I could see was the bed. I slid under the crisp white sheets, feeling the coolness embrace me. I didn't move until that evening.

Even though Brewster County is the second largest county in the lower United States, news traveled like lightning. My first thought when I woke up was that Noah would have heard about everything, and that I needed to find him and tell him myself.

I walked into the tiled shower and stood there, letting the hot water seep into every pore, willing it to make me feel clean and wash away all trace of the last forty-eight hours. When I finally got out, in a hurry now to find Noah, clothes were waiting for me on the side chair, just as the crises center lady had promised. Friends were waiting in the hall, and when I opened my door, they came in to hug and offer help. It felt weird immediately.

They had such sorrowful looks on their faces. Tears were rolling down the cheek of another. I felt a gush of pity wash over me.

"Stop that!" I ordered. It seemed imperative that I had control. "Do you know where Noah is?" I asked, willing my voice to sound authoritative.

"He's still at his friend Tony's house, and Tony's mom has offered to look after him until you can pick him up ... and there's no hurry," one of the friends offered. I was relieved. I asked them to take me to a hotel room, where I could rest and think until I figured out what to do next. Going back to my house in Terlingua wasn't an option.

They told me the guy had been apprehended in Mexico and was waiting with Texas law enforcement on the Mexico side of the river. They said that by dawn, most of Terlingua and South County had heard bits and pieces of what had happened, and had gathered as a group on the Texas side of the river. It looked like a true, "Mexican Standoff."

The problem was, Texas officials had no authority to bring the guy back to the United States. Texas has no extradition treaty with Mexico. Ever since there had even been a border, lawbreakers on both sides would do their crimes, then race to their home country before apprehension. This was the same song, different verse ... my verse. Mexico officials were waiting for permission to hand him over to Texas officials. Meanwhile, the guy was handcuffed to an old truck on the banks of the Mexican side of the river. One of my friends mentioned that the residents gathered on the Texas side were talking about just shooting him from across the river. Others, more level headed, insisted he would surely be brought back to Texas to stand trial. As the morning wore on, the crowd grew. Finally, by mid-morning the Mexican officials told the Texas lawmen that they would not be returning him to Texas. They had orders from "higher up" that he was to be taken to the nearest town, Ojinaga, and await further instructions. When the Texas officials came back to the Texas side and told the crowd what was going to, happen, taunts and jeers were screamed across the river. Threats were made, but after he was removed from the area by Mexican officials, the crowd on the Texas side began to disperse too.

He had left my truck on the Texas side of the river, with just a few dings and scratches from the brush. It was a brand-new truck, I had only made one payment on it, and I felt stranded without my own transportation. "Billy Pat said as soon as the law enforcement officials had processed it, you could get your truck back," my friend Charlie said, and handed me a $100 bill to pay for the room. "Take care," he said with a sorrowful look as he turned to go.

I knew people cared about me, but being pitied is a hard emotion to swallow. I wanted my strength back. I couldn't stand looking into friends' eyes and seeing their heartfelt concern because it made me feel like a victim. Even in my tired and weakened state I felt like the victor ... I had survived. I didn't want pity, I wanted the guy brought to Texas and brought to trial. Forgiving him didn't mean I had forgotten what he had done. I wanted to face him in a court of law. Naively I thought that if he faced consequences for his actions, my world of normalcy would somehow return.

I walked into my motel room, still exhausted, and had to make a few phone calls. I called my relief clerk to make sure she could work the following day at the post office. I called my boss in El Paso to tell them I wouldn't be back to work anytime soon, and, briefly, why. I called a friend and asked her to pick Noah up at Tony's and bring him to me. I called my brother and told him, in a rush of words, what had happened. I asked him to call my father for me. I couldn't bear to repeat the story another time and I couldn't bear to hear my father blame me for all that had happened.

All the immediate work done, I lay on the bed staring at the ceiling. I felt like I was behind a translucent veil, like there was glass between me and the world. Every muscle in my body ached, and I just wanted to feel "normal" again.

I fell asleep again, trying to figure out what to do next. I woke up to loud knocking on the door. "Who is it?" I yelled. No answer. The room was dim and I could tell it was almost night. "Who's there?" I yelled again, and still no answer. "Tell me who you are! Tell me who you are!" I screamed, not quite awake or fully conscious, I only felt fear ... again. Walking to the door I yelled again to find out who was there, and this time my son answered in a small voice, "It's me, Mom. It's me." I unlocked the door and grabbed him, so happy to see him, so grateful he had not been home that horrible night. We were both crying.

My friend Barbara had picked him up and, standing behind him, asked if she could come in. We sat down at the small table and she began explaining that she had stopped by my house after picking Noah up. "That awful yellow 'crime scene' tape is all over the entryway," she said, "and I had a hell of a time convincing the deputy to let me in. He gave me five minutes to gather some of your belongings, so I dumped as much as I could into a bag to bring it to you. I did remember your toothbrush, makeup, and a few clothes, just whatever I could grab in a hurry. I probably missed a ton of things you need," she continued, "I'm sorry."

A true friend, Barbara had had her share of troubles, too. She had faced the death of her only two sons and had only one grandson left. A career educator, she was matter of fact, and down to earth, and I saw no pity in her eyes. She just wanted to help in any practical way she could. She was acting stern, to keep from crying.

"Don't go home, Jayson," she said. "Everything is a mess and has fingerprint dust all over. Stay here for a while and don't worry about your house. Really, you don't want to be there." She had even brought hamburgers with her, and Noah was already devouring his sitting in front of the television, a rare treat for him.

I thanked her profusely and after bringing in the bag of items she had gathered from my house, she left. Noah and I sat together and ate our hamburgers, watching tv.

Finally, I turned off the television and told Noah I wanted to talk to him. He was hesitant to say anything, and when I questioned him about what he had heard he said simply, "I don't want to talk about it." Even though it probably wasn't healthy for him to keep all his feelings to himself, I couldn't help but feel relieved. How do you talk to a 10-year-old about this kind of stuff? Putting my questions aside, I decided that being together, and safe, would suffice for now. We could deal with the impact later.

16

Learning to Live Again

THE NEXT DAY OFFICERS BROUGHT my truck to me and gave me an update on the guy's fate. He was to stay in Mexico. Mexican officials would not let Texas extradite him for trial. Mexico would try him. They were unable to tell me when or where the trial would be held.

I was devastated. "What kinds of rights do women in Mexico have?" I wondered. The stereotype "machismo" of Mexican men would surely apply in any court of Mexican law. Maybe they would just let him go. After all, it happened in Texas and maybe they would believe him and not me ... if I even got to testify.

I started to feel like a victim again. "All this devastation in my life, my whole world turned upside down, and now he doesn't even have to go to trial in Texas for what he did?" I couldn't believe it. This was not right. This was not fair. This was yet another outrage.

The officer tried to calm me down. "You have been summoned to the magistrate in Ojinaga, Mexico, to tell officials there what has happened," he said. "They want to hear your side of the story."

Incredulous, I almost yelled, "What? Now I have to go THERE instead of him coming HERE to pay for what he did?"

The officer tried again to calm me. "Yes, but we will be with you. You don't have to go alone. The Sheriff and I will both be with you, as well as the deputy for Terlingua. His wife is a Mexican national and he speaks perfect Spanish. He'll be our interpreter." His words did have a calming effect, as I tried to convince myself that it was a positive thing that Mexican officials wanted to hear my side of the story.

"Okay," I finally said, "when are we supposed to go?"

"Next week," he said, "and we'll pick you up and drive there in a Sheriff's marked car."

He paused and then, looking a bit uncertain, asked, "Now, I'm sorry but I have to ask you. You don't have a handgun, do you? We will not be allowed to take any guns into Mexico. Even the Sheriff and the deputies will have to leave their weapons in Texas. You understand that, don't you?"

I nodded that I understood, at the same time making a mental note to buy a gun. "I could leave the gun in my handbag. They're not going to search me. When they bring the bastard into the interrogation room, I can just shoot him myself," I thought with what seemed like perfectly logical reasoning.

"Unless there's a change, we'll pick you up next Monday about 8:00, and we'll all drive to Ojinaga together. Will that be all right with you?" he asked.

I nodded that I'd be ready, and asked if I could now go back to my house to get some more clothes and a few items for Noah. He said the house had been "processed" and it was perfectly all right for me to go home.

I had already decided I could not go home to stay, at least not for a while. I would have to rent an apartment in town. Noah needed to be enrolled in school. I needed more clothes, I needed things from my house.

The next few days were a whirlwind of activity. I started by taking Noah to school to get him enrolled. He was taken to a classroom, while I met with the counselor. I introduced myself, and she said simply, "I know who you are," sparing me the trauma of yet again telling why we were in Alpine and why Noah was changing schools from Terlingua. With the same pitying look in her eyes, she tried to reassure me that they understood that Noah may have some trouble getting adjusted to a new school, considering the circumstances. I thanked her, filled out some paperwork, and left.

Next, I needed to find an apartment. I knew that Billy Pat and his wife kept an apartment in town, even though he was the constable in Terlingua. It was near the college and I decided that of all the places I could be, living next door to him would be perfect. I found the manager of the apartments and asked if one was available close to Billy Pat's. I explained I didn't know how long I would need the apartment and didn't want to sign a long lease. The manager, again with the same sorrowful look, said she understood. She showed me an apartment a few doors down from where Billy Pat's was. Made of cinderblock, the rooms were stark but serviceable. Although they were all one-bedroom apartments, this one had an extra room between the living room and my bedroom ... perfect as a room for Noah. I signed the short lease, went to my bank to withdraw some money, and paid her for it in cash.

Things can happen quickly in a small town. The telephone company is local and easy to apply for a new phone. The other utilities were already on and included in the lease. Now all I needed was some furniture.

I called my friend Barbara and asked her if she and her husband could meet me at my house the next day, to help me pack. Always willing to help, she asked if there was anything else they could do.

"Not that I can think of right now," I said, "but you're the first person I'll call if I do."

It was time to pick Noah up from school, gas up my truck, go get dinner somewhere, and make a list of everything I wanted to get out of my house. I told Noah that I had rented an apartment for us and his first question was, "Does it have a television?" Laughing, I said it did, and suddenly realized how out of touch we had been, living in Terlingua. I asked him if he had made new friends in school and he was excited to tell me he did. "I met a kid and he and I look just alike!" he squealed, and then followed with, "well, ALMOST just alike. I'll show him to you tomorrow when you take me to school. His name is Steve, and we're in the same class. He lives on a ranch and even has his own horse!" he said with excitement.

"How amazing is that," I thought, my mind wandering back to memories of the ranch, and the summer I shared with Trey. If things had been different, Noah would have attended this school for years and been friends with this little boy the whole time. None of this would have happened, and this school year for Noah would have been just another school year. He would have happily been Trey's stepson and by now well versed in all the chores of the ranch. And he would have had his own horse, too. Another layer of sadness seemed to fall around my shoulders, and I tried to paste a smile on my face so that Noah wouldn't notice

"Thank God Trey's not in town," I thought, knowing that if he were, he would do something to get revenge for me, even if it was wrong, even if it was dangerous. Hopefully it will be months before he even hears about this. I had heard that Trey had gone to work in the oilfields, to try and pull the ranch out of debt. I prayed that he would NEVER hear about all of this. That was one prayer that went unanswered.

The next day I took Noah to school and headed down highway 118 to Terlingua. I was feeling stressed, alone, and not quite sure if I should be going back by myself. What would I feel when I walked into that house? What would I remember with sudden and frightening emotions? "Thank God for Barbara," I thought, "I just couldn't do this alone."

I drove up the driveway to my house and sat for a few moments in my truck. The yellow crime scene tape was gone, but the door into the courtyard was standing ajar. "I guess there have been plenty of people in and out of the house," I thought. "Someone just forgot to latch it."

Climbing out of my truck I walked down the flagstone sidewalk to the main part of the house. Nothing was locked and I walked into the living-dining room. The wooden dining table was covered in a fine, black silt. Some of it had dropped onto the flagstone floor, and a few footprints were etched into the dust. The kitchen counter was covered in the same fine silt, as well as my desk in my office. I gathered enough courage to walk into the dressing room-bath room and, sure enough, the fine silt covered the counter and the handles on the sink.

Everywhere I looked reminded me of some horrible scene of that fateful night. Breathing hard and breaking out in a cold sweat, I decided to start gathering a few clothes, some personal items, and a few things Noah had asked for. Walking into Noah's room, I was surprised to see that his desk was also covered in the black silt, and even the headboard of his bed. Even though it would be a mess to clean the house, I was glad the officers had done such a thorough job.

I dreaded going into my bedroom, but there were things I needed in there. I walked out of Noah's room and across the deck to the door of my bedroom. Pausing, my heart beating wildly, I opened the door and stood there. With a terrifying and blinding memory, I suddenly remembered seeing eyes through the tiny crack of the open door. It was a subconscious seeing, a picture just below consciousness that your brain doesn't register. I had seen his eyes that night but didn't recognize what I was seeing. "That's why I felt someone was watching me," I thought, frozen with the same fear I had felt that night. "I felt it because it was him, standing deathly still behind the door," I thought with a sudden and sickening feeling.

"How could I have missed that?" my mind screamed. "If I had really seen him maybe none of this would have happened!" my anguished thoughts continued. Ready to burst into tears, I caught myself again, and pushed the thoughts, and the sorrow, and the fear out of my mind. "Get what you think you need and get out of here," I said to myself, and at the same time heard the gravel of a truck driving into the driveway. Looking out, I saw Barbara and her husband pulling into the drive. Once their vehicle stopped, with characteristic control, Barbara stormed out of the truck and walked up to me.

"What are you doing here by yourself?" she demanded. "I told you to wait for us!"

"I know you did," I said, "and I'm sorry. I didn't know it would be this bad," I finished.

"Well tell me what else you want and then go get in your truck. I can do the rest. You don't need to be here," she said with all the authoritative drive a schoolteacher and principal could muster. Friends for years, she and her husband had careers as teachers and lately, a middle school principal. "Hell, nothing's gonna scare me," she said, "I'm a teacher!" And with that she marched me out to my truck and a few minutes later returned with all the kitchen utensils I would need, and a set of silverware and china. Her husband followed with sheets, towels, and clothes.

"That ought to do it," she exclaimed, placing things in the back of my truck. "If you need anything else, just call me and I can bring it into town for you."

"And that's what friends are for," I thought, "real friends who stand by you no matter what." I felt a wave of gratitude fall over me, as I realized that at least some positive things were coming out of this whole ordeal. I started my truck, and headed back to town. I would be just in time to pick Noah up from school.

17

Going to Mexico

THE NEXT FEW DAYS WERE busy with moving my things into the new apartment, meeting Noah's new friends, and helping him get settled. Never one to share any of his feelings with me, he seemed to be happy and adjusting to his new class and new teacher. I had scheduled a meeting with the only psychiatrist in town, a woman, thank God. We were to meet the following week, and I wanted to have Noah see her at least a few times. Maybe he would open up to her.

As the day to go to Mexico drew closer, so did my apprehension. "I hate having to tell the whole thing again," I worried. "Going through everything again just makes me feel worse than I already do. And what's the point? Can't they just listen to the tape made at the hospital?" I fumed.

I made arrangements for Noah to be picked up after school, in case we weren't back in time, and got ready for the trip.

I knew it was wrong, but I didn't care. I had bought a gun, and had been carrying it with me in my handbag for days. Even though I didn't know a thing about guns, somehow it made me feel safer. Betting that no one would search me, either in Texas or Mexico,

I slipped it into my handbag. I convinced myself that the deputies and the sheriff carried guns hidden somewhere on them. At least, I hoped they did. I had no reason to trust that the Mexican officials would be anything but corrupt.

True to their word, the Sheriff and a deputy picked me up at 8:00 Monday morning. I climbed in the back of the car, and we began the hundred mile trip, making small talk. I was trying to keep my mind off the coming interrogation. I think they just felt awkward, and I winced inside at the thought of how they would feel on the ride back to Alpine after hearing the story.

Awkward, sad and full of pity. I could recognize those feelings in people from a mile away. I could hardly go to the grocery store without meeting someone's gaze full of those emotions. I yearned for the time when people who knew me would just offer a cheerful "Hi! How ya doin?" and place me in some other identity ... Noah's mom, the Postmaster of Terlingua, a songwriter, ANYTHING but "victim".

Finally, we all ran out of small talk, and the Sheriff started to, gently, tell me how the whole "interview", as he called it, would probably unfold. "I don't know if they will actually bring in the guy and have you tell your story in front of him, but I wouldn't be surprised," the Sheriff started. "Just try to keep your cool and don't get outwardly upset. These fellas are pretty big muckity mucks in the city of Ojinaga, and they're used to folks catering to 'em," he divulged.

"I'll do my best," was all I could say, with a million thoughts swirling in my head. "I've been around Mexican culture most of my life ... I know how men are. I won't try to antagonize them, but who knows what's going to happen?" I offered. "You know what I'm talking about, Sheriff. Blond haired, blue-eyed women who get themselves into a bad situation and then expect the law to get after some poor guy. I won't let them make HIM the one who's hurt in this deal. I know what he did, he knows what he did, and they can damn well accept what I tell them at face value. I will not stand for them making me to blame, I can tell you that," I blurted out. And then I was embarrassed for talking so bold and tough. "If she's was so tough, how did any of this happen anyway?" I was sure they were thinking.

We drove on in silence for a little while. We were going really fast, almost eighty-five miles an hour, maybe faster. The trip didn't take long, and before I knew it, we were parked near the international bridge that connects Presidio, Texas with Ojinaga, Mexico. The small dusty town of Presidio looked even smaller with Ojinaga just across the river. A city of probably twenty-five thousand people, not counting the surrounding area, it was the nearest "city" to every town in Brewster County. Practically everybody in Terlingua went there at least every other week for fresh avocados, limes, tortillas and other grocery items. But they were renowned for their avocados.

We'd go to the market and pick out the ones we wanted. Then at the counter someone would cut it in half, take out the seed, and put half a lime face down in its place. Then it would be wrapped in plastic or tin foil, weighed, and you paid and were out the door. The shopkeepers and locals were more than friendly ... they were glad to see tourists with American dollars. We'd buy tequila or vodka, and generally make a day of it. With several great restaurants, we'd eat a huge lunch, then drive leisurely back to Terlingua. It was a ritual. It was required. It was south county protocol.

As the three of us sat there looking at Mexico, the Sheriff started to speak again. "Okay guys, one more time," he started. "If you have a gun or weapon of any kind, now's the time to turn it in to customs/border control over there. Deputy?" and he looked over to the deputy riding in the passenger seat.

"Yessir, I've already got mine off and ready to turn in," the deputy quickly replied.

The sheriff twisted his body to turn around and look at me in the back seat. He didn't say anything, he just looked at me. I looked back and neither one of us chose to insult the other with a question that would only be answered with a lie. Finally, he said, "Wait here," and he and the deputy walked across the highway and disappeared into the Customs Office. I waited.

Within minutes they came back to the car. "All right then, here we go!" the Sheriff said, and we drove slowly across the rickety international bridge. Stopping at the inspection station on the Mexico side, the Sheriff and officer spoke briefly in Spanish. The officer stuck his head in the window and looked at me in the back seat. The Sheriff stated the name of the man we were going to see, and the officer waved us through.

We drove to the municipal building almost in the center of town. The concrete building, bigger than any building in Alpine, echoed as we walked inside and asked where the office was. The woman looked stern, but directed us to a nearby stairway and simply said, "Second floor."

My stomach felt upset and I had a lightheaded feeling. I talked sternly to myself, trying to bolster my courage for the coming ordeal. We stopped outside in the hallway, in front of the door of the office we were looking for. Looking down at me the Sheriff asked, "Are you okay?" And there it was. The look. The sadness. The pity. The concern.

I wanted to impress him that I was more than just, "Okay." I wanted to be strong and bold and ready. "Oh yes," I answered, staring straight into his eyes. "I'm looking forward to this!"

He nodded and knocked on the door. We walked into the cavernous concrete room. A panel of 3 men sat on folding chairs behind a long table. There were 4 folding chairs placed in front of them, and one man motioned for us to sit down.

"Oh great," I thought. "Not a female in sight except me. Why didn't I think to bring the counselor from the Crisis Center with us? This is going to be horrible."

Deputy Klingemann began speaking in Spanish. He introduced each of us, and thanked the magistrates for seeing us. He told them he would be our interpreter, and if they had any questions to stop him at any time. The magistrates nodded their approval and waved for me to begin talking.

I started telling them where I was when the attack began and why I was outside. I continued with what had happened until one of the men stopped me abruptly.

"What were you wearing?" one man asked.

"I was wearing jeans and a T-shirt," I answered dutifully, wondering why that mattered.

"NO! You were wearing a blouse with buttons on the front!" he said forcefully. Although I didn't recognize all the words he used, there was no mistaking his tone and the sneer on his face.

I looked questioningly at Deputy Klingemann and he told me in English to go on with my account.

"What is his name?" one man asked.

"He didn't tell me his real name. He told me to call him 'Te Amo' and so I did. That's the only name I know him by," I explained. All of the men looked surprised and I wasn't sure why. I had not thought of what the name meant the entire night of terror. There were obviously too many other things to occupy my thoughts. It still didn't dawn on me. And so I continued with what had transpired throughout the night, using the name "Te Amo", that he had told me to call him.

I turned to Deputy Klingemann and asked him what the name

meant in English. He answered simply, "My love." I was sickened by the psychopathic trick the guy had played on me. Kidnapping me, torturing me, raping me, all the while calling him "my love" was like pouring salt into a wound.

I went on with the recount of everything that had happened that night. Not wanting to reveal every sexual indecency I had experienced, many times my voice would trail off, leaving words and acts unsaid. At those points Deputy Klingemann would finish my sentences in Spanish, leaving nothing to the magistrates' imagination.

Still calling him "Te Amo" I would tell them what I could of the story, and tried to make sure they knew the remoteness and desolation of the area where all of this had happened. I didn't want them to think Terlingua was like Ojinaga ... a town with houses and people everywhere. I wanted them to know that Te Amo had attacked me in the vast emptiness of the desert, sure that no one would catch him.

"YOU WILL NOT CALL HIM THAT!" one Magistrate suddenly screamed. "YOU WILL NEVER USE THAT TERM AGAIN!" He continued, punctuating his sentence with short jabs into the air. "His name is Refugio Gardea Gonzalez! Use that name!" he commanded.

Even though I felt like screaming, myself, at the indignity the bastard's name had forced on me, the four of us were stunned at the magistrate's outburst. He continued his angry tirade by asking, "Doesn't she have any brothers? A father? THEY are supposed to be taking care of this, NOT US!" he yelled, this time slapping a folder of paperwork against the ancient typewriter sitting in front of him.

Now my own anger was beginning to surface. Anger focused not only at Refugio Gardea Gonzalez, but also at being treated like a liar by the magistrates. Now they were impugning my family, foisting the expectations of their own culture onto me and my culture. Losing my temper, I looked at Deputy Klingemann and told him to translate my next words exactly.

"This man, this Refugio Gardea Gonzalez is a monster," I started in a low voice, getting out of my chair and standing before them. "He did everything I said he did and more. Your culture obviously dismisses such crimes as insignificant." My voice rising now, I continued, "He needs to be brought to trial and pay for his crimes! That's not going to happen in this piece of shit country where you depend on a woman's family to correct the crimes against her! Let us extradite him to Texas!" I yelled.

And that, as they say, is when the party started.

18

Letting Go

THE SHERIFF AND HIS TWO deputies stood up, and one by one so did
the magistrates. The Sheriff nodded to Deputy Klingemann, and
told him to say our farewells to the magistrates, and thank them
for their time. No doubt my hysterical tirade confirmed their low
opinion of a woman who would "allow" such things to happen. My
worst fears seemed to be confirmed: this bastard would never face
trial in an American court.

We walked out of the building, and got back in the Sheriff's car.
"They're not going to do a damn thing," I said with fire in my voice.

"Well, you just never know about these things. Their judgment
probably isn't the last word. No doubt there are higher-ups who will
get to rule on his extradition. We'll just have to wait and see," the
Sheriff said, obviously trying to speak with a non-judgmental voice
to help calm me down. Feeling guilty now, I felt I owed an apology
to the him.

"I hope you're right, Sheriff," I started, then added, "I'm sorry
I lost my temper in there. I really can't explain what happened or
why their words hit me so hard. It's one thing for them to believe
that basically I'm a whore, but quite another to say things against

my family. Anyway, I'm sorry I blew up. I hope I didn't embarrass you."

I sat back in the seat and decided to try and enjoy the ride home. The beautiful country once again flying by my window helped to give rise to some much-needed introspection.

"This temper thing is getting to be a habit," I thought. "Why do I fly off the handle so often and so ferociously? I feel like I don't have any control of anything anymore." I decided to bring it up with the psychiatrist at my first visit later that week.

We were back in Alpine with plenty of time to pick Noah up from school. I thanked the Sheriff and the deputy when they dropped me off at my apartment, climbed into my truck and drove to the school. I was about 20 minutes early, so I used the time to just sit quietly in my truck and think. I made a mental list of what I would talk to the psychiatrist about, and questions I wanted to ask her. I remembered we were out of groceries for supper and Noah's breakfast so reminded myself to stop at the grocery store on the way home. Then I remembered Noah had invited his new friend, Steve, over after school. I added treats to the groceries I had in mind.

A million other "to-do's" crowded my thoughts and momentarily I was overwhelmed with all that needed to be done. Mercifully the school dismissal bell rung, and kids came running out of the building, Noah and Steve among them. They ran to the truck and climbed in, with Noah saying in a rush, "Hi Mom, this is Steve."

"I'm pleased to meet you, Steve. And you and Noah really DO resemble each other!" I added amused at the coincidence. "Are you boys acting all right in your classes?" I asked, wanting to sound like a mom, and not like a zombie, the way I felt.

"Yes, Ma'm," Steve answered, carefully polite. Noah, on the other hand, just couldn't resist. "No, Mom, we cut up all the time and have detention half the day!" he laughed.

"Uh huh," I countered. "How about I let you guys out at the park to work out some of that energy while I go to the grocery store? I'll get you something to snack on, too, any requests?" I finished.

Both boys brightened at the mention of food and Noah said, "Just get some stuff to make sandwiches with. And chips. And those pizza bites are good. And maybe something to drink?" he asked, almost begging, knowing I didn't allow for many sodas.

"Be back at the apartment in an hour or less," I said as I let them out at the park. "I'll have some food ready by then." I went on to the grocery store, and almost crawled out of the truck.

"I'm so tired," I thought, "I feel like I've run a marathon and then got hit by a train. Why am I so tired?"

I remembered to brace myself to face the pitying faces I was sure to encounter in the store. "After this many weeks you'd think people would have forgotten by now," I thought. "Or at least have forgotten what the 'poor victim' looks like. Is this ever going to end? Will I ever feel 'normal' again?"

I shook myself back to reality. "I don't have time for this crap," I thought. "Go get the food, go home and fix the kids something to eat. Worry about this later."

The boys, tired and sweaty, were already home when I got there. I hurriedly put some sandwiches together, put the pizza bites in the microwave, and poured coke into icy glasses. They sat on the living room floor and turned on the television, loud, drowning out my thoughts.

I busied myself in the kitchen, putting away groceries, getting something started for dinner, washing dishes. With a knock on the door, Steve's dad appeared to pick him up and take him home. We introduced ourselves, I said good-bye to Steve, and then told Noah to get started on his homework. I took some laundry downstairs to the washroom and stayed there until the clothes were washed, dried, and folded. We ate supper, watched a little tv, and then it was, mercifully, time for bed.

As I sunk into the soft mattress my thoughts wandered in and out of the events of the day, especially the events in Mexico. The realization that this exhaustion was now my life, that the men sitting in judgement of me didn't believe me, that I was powerless to do anything about it overwhelmed me. There in the darkness I recounted everything I had lost: my home, my job, my reputation, and my money. Money was already an issue and I worried it was going to become more of one. Without working I was now living on my savings. What would I do when that ran out? The post office had put me on leave, but that would run out soon too.

My thoughts swirled and twisted around in my head, in a loop that always ended in the same place. "I have no money, no job, no place to live, and a child to raise. What am I going to do?" I worried.

The exhaustion and the depression closed in on me and I began to cry. I decided to, finally, let myself cry. The tears streamed down my face in torrents, wetting my pillow. The cries became deep, uncensored sobs, and my body began shaking and heaving with every sound. I was lost in the pain, in the sorrow, in the fear, in the worry. Everything was only black.

19

Counseling

My FIRST VISIT WITH THE psychiatrist, Dr. Sanchez, was scheduled for the next day. Torn between feeling like I was at death's door, and wanting to appear capable and in control, I tried to get myself together for our meeting. I'd never been to a "shrink" before, and harbored some of the usual stereotypes.

"Maybe I'll get some rest just lying on her couch," I thought. "I never seem to be able to feel rested no matter how long I sleep."

"I wonder if she'll delve back into my childhood," I wondered, "and wouldn't that be a field day!" as I remembered some of the trials and tribulations of growing up with narcissist parents, too many siblings and never enough money.

As it turned out, of course, my sessions with Dr. Sanchez were nothing like I had imagined. Her office was in part of her house, and when I walked in, I liked her immediately.

She greeted me warmly and ushered me into her working space. From reading the newspapers and contact with the crisis center, she was already well acquainted with everything that had happened. Thankfully I didn't have to start from the beginning of the ordeal.

She told me that, other than death of a close family member, I had suffered 4 of the 5 major stressors in life ... all at the same time ... rape, kidnapping, loss of job, loss of home. "What are you doing to cope with all of this?" she asked, and then noted, "You seem to be taking care of your physical needs. I understand you live here in Alpine, now. You've enrolled your son in school and you have him with you. Frankly, I'm in awe of your strength and stamina."

"I don't know how I'm doing or what I'm doing," I answered, feeling like a fraud because I had evidently fooled even a trained doctor. "To be honest, though, I don't think I'm as strong as I appear. I flinch at every loud sound. I can't vacuum or do anything that would mask sound without wearing my gun. I check the locks on the doors and windows several times at night, 'just to be sure'. I worry this guy will get out of jail in Mexico and come looking for me. And ... I'm running out of money. I'm starting to think I'll have to go back to my house because I can't pay rent forever. I don't know what I'm going to do about my job. As far as what I do to 'cope', I suppose I just stay as busy as possible. When I'm alone, I cry. And I try to think of ways to make things easier for Noah. I know he misses his life in Terlingua."

She listened intently and we discussed various techniques to address all of my issues. She said she was diagnosing me with PTSD, and explained what that was. "Post-Traumatic Stress Disorder, or PTSD, is a psychological disorder that can occur whenever a person has experienced an unexpected, dangerous, or scary event. Fear triggers the chemicals in your body to signal the 'fight or flee' response to one of those events. There is a range of reactions people can experience during and after a traumatic event, but most people recover from these reactions. If symptoms persist over a long period of time, months or even years, and interfere with normal daily activities, you probably have PTSD. The extent of your symptoms indicates to me that you do, indeed, have this condition. But I will also tell you that, after listening to the tape of your recounting of the events of that night, that you are also very resilient, and possess an exceptional level of thought processing. Rape is not considered a mild psychosocial stressor, but coupled with prolonged detention and continuous threat to your life it can be thought of as a catastrophic impairment. I would be worried about you if you DIDN'T have PTSD. It doesn't go away," she said, "but it usually does get better."

Our hour was up and she ended by telling me to call her if I had any new concerns, or if I just wanted to talk. She reassured me that she thought I was doing all that I possibly could, and that, one of these days, everything would calm down. We made a schedule for future visits, and she showed me out the back door. "It's a private exit," she said, noticing my surprised look. "It's no one's business that you come to see me, and when you leave by this door, no one can see you. It's a matter of privacy." I was grateful for the concern she showed for her clients by setting up her office this way. In a small town, gossip is currency. Whoever has the latest "scoop" has the most currency and credibility. I grew up in a small town similar to Alpine, and I know how these things work. And right now, my situation seemed to be the hottest topic in town.

"Thank you" I said as I opened the door to leave. "You are most perceptive and kind." And with that I returned to my silent apartment to wait until it was time for school to be out, time to pick Noah up, and time to pretend for a few hours that everything was "normal".

20

Making Plans

THE THANKSGIVING AND CHRISTMAS HOLIDAYS passed with little enthusiasm on my part. Noah and I did put up a small Christmas tree, and of course Santa somehow found our new apartment. I still felt that I was caught in some sort of vortex of unreality. Trying to act like everything was normal didn't bring normalcy, it only served to enhance the feeling of disconnection. As each day blended into the next, I felt caught in a never changing loop. I was growing desperate for something to change. I needed for Mexico to decide what they were going to do with Gonzalez.

To my knowledge neither law enforcement nor I had received any news as to when, or if, Refugio Gardea Gonzalez would stand trial in Mexico. All I knew was that he was still incarcerated in the Ojinaga jail. Well, I didn't really KNOW he was still in Ojinaga, but since I had heard nothing to the contrary, I BELIEVED he was still there. If that was true, then we were both existing in a sort of limbo world.

I realized I didn't know anything about him except his name and the name of the small town in Mexico where his family lived and he had grown up. I didn't know his age, I didn't know his past, I didn't know anything except the monster I saw him as. Since I wasn't getting any satisfaction from the Mexican judicial system, I finally decided to take action of my own, even if what I found out couldn't play any part in court proceedings ... if there ever were "court proceedings". "I don't have to wait here and feel helpless to impact my own case against him," I reasoned, "I need to know who he is." I started to plan a trip into Mexico and take things into my own hands.

I had a good friend who spoke fluent Spanish and I convinced her to go with me to Mexico. I wanted to see where this monster had grown up. I wanted to speak with his parents and friends, to see what kind of person he was. I wanted to know everything about him.

I began to get everything in order. I arranged for Noah to stay with his friend, Steve, for a few days. Steve's parents assured me it would be no trouble, and said they were glad to help. I took my truck to the shop and had the oil changed and everything checked out. I didn't want any vehicle problems in Mexico. I planned to be gone only for about 3 or 4 days; a day to get there, a day to get back, and a day or two to "poke around". I postponed an appointment with Dr. Sanchez, drew some money out of my savings, and by the end of the week, we were ready to go.

Just planning the trip gave me new energy. At last I was being PROactive instead of REactive. I was making the plan on my own. I wasn't asking anyone's permission, and I didn't inform the Sheriff of what I was going to do. It was exhilarating.

"Maybe I'll actually get information that can help in getting him extradited," I hoped. "SOME information is better than NONE," I reasoned. I wasn't afraid to go to Mexico. I'd been there many times. It wasn't MEXICO that had done me harm, it was one single person from Mexico. And that person was Refugio Gardea Gonzalez." I was on a mission.

We left early on Sunday morning, driving straight from Alpine to Presidio, crossing the international bridge and heading straight for Chihuahua City, about one hundred miles from Ojinaga. We had no trouble at the aduana getting into Mexico. We asked for a visa for only five days, saying we were on vacation. It's a bit unusual for women to travel alone in Mexico, and Sara and I went over various precautions we would take. First of all, stay together at all times we decided; every break, every restaurant, every motel, we would be a pair. Second, even if we had a lead on someone with information, we would not go into the countryside. We could meet in town, or do without the information. And, last but not least, no drinking, not even in our motel room.

We had been friends for a long time, and we filled the hours of driving catching up. I had been fairly reclusive since "the big event" and hadn't really shared anything about that night with anyone other than law enforcement and Dr. Sanchez. She wanted to know everything so I filled in the "highlights" of that fateful night in the course of telling her what I wanted to find out from Gonzalez's family and friends. I thought it would be best to just initiate a conversation and see what, if anything, would come of it.

Late that evening we reached his small town and checked into the better looking of two hotels. Our room was sparse, but clean. The tile floors were waxed, the twin beds nicely made, and the room had windows looking out onto the courtyard filled with tropical plants. Outside the courtyard and across the street was a small restaurant. Perfect.

We both took showers and dropped into bed. Sara stayed up and read, I was too exhausted to do anything but fall asleep thinking about what tomorrow would bring. The next thing I knew, it was a beautiful sunny morning.

Excited to try and find anyone who knew him or his family, we dressed quickly and dashed across the street to the little restaurant. Over coffee and pancakes, we started talking to the waitress. We said a friend of ours, Refugio Gonzalez, was in jail in Ojinaga, and wondered if she knew him or his family. We said we didn't really know why he was in jail, but that Texas was trying to extradite him to the United States. We just wanted to help.

With a surprised look on her face, she said she knew him. "I hope he isn't in too much trouble," she said. "He's only twenty-three or twenty-four. I think he's been in trouble before."

Sara asked if she knew where his parents lived, if they were still living. "Oh si, si, viven aqui," she answered and said she would write down their address. "They are pretty old," she remembered, "and I haven't seen them for quite a while. But I'm sure they still live here," and she walked away to get a pen and paper.

I could barely finish my coffee. Trying to act like it was no big deal, we paid and left a pretty hefty tip. "We're staying in the hotel just across the street," Sara said, "so if anybody else knows him and wants to talk to us, that's where we are." Taking the slip of paper, we thanked her and hurried across the street.

"Do you think we should go this early?" I asked Sara. "If they're old, maybe they're still in bed. It's only 8:00."

We decided to wait until 9:00, then drive around looking for the street. If we couldn't find it, we'd stop and ask directions. It would give us something to do.

We walked back to the hotel, made our beds, and, even though we thought we would stay another night, packed our belongings to take with us. We loaded the car, and a few minutes before 9:00, took off.

Riding around town was strange. It was small, with a population I would guess to be around 2,000. It was just off a main highway, though, which accounted for the amenities a town this size in

Mexico would have. There were three gas stations and we stopped at one to fill the tank. The attendant seemed nice enough and to save time we showed him the paper and asked if he knew the way to that address.

In rapid Spanish, he told us two different ways to get there. I was never more grateful that Sara was so proficient in Spanish. I would never have been able to do this by myself. We paid and left, and drove directly to Gonzalez's parents address.

It was a small house, close to the western edge of town, a few blocks off the main street. There were few windows in the house, and the roof was made of tin. The front of the house was bare dirt, swept clean. Sitting in the car, gathering our courage, we talked about how it would have been growing up here, and in that house. There was an adobe wall in front of the house, reaching around to the east side. Two tall trees stood in front of the house, behind the wall. A stone walk went to the door, and the door was standing open.

"I take that as a good sign," I said quietly, "a welcoming sign. Let's try our luck." We both got out of the car and walked across the street, stepping just inside the small courtyard. Sara called out, "Hola! Hello! Hello to the house!" a simple greeting that was common. It was more polite than walking right up to the door, especially since the door was wide open. A woman who appeared to be about sixty-five or seventy years old stepped just inside the door. "Yes?" she asked, "how can I help you?"

She was dressed plainly, with an apron tied around her waist. Her hair was neatly pulled back into a bun and deep wrinkles were etched into her face. We established that she was Gonzalez's mother, and said that we wished to speak with her and her husband about their son, Refugio. The half-smile on his mother's face faded, and she pulled her apron up over her face before she turned away, muttering something we couldn't quite hear. His father stepped into the courtyard, and with a tired voice, said, "What has he done now?"

Sara explained as briefly as possible that he was in jail in Ojinaga.

"We knew already that something was wrong," he replied, "when he stopped sending money orders. I'm not sure I want to know, but tell me, please, what happened?" he asked slowly and with a deep voice.

Sara said only that he had attacked a woman in Texas and had been apprehended after he crossed the river back into Mexico. She said it was unclear whether he would be extradited to Texas, or face trial in Mexico.

"Not again," Mr. Gonzalez fairly moaned, "not again." He took off his sweat stained hat and wiped his brow with a large piece of cloth, as much to hide his face as to wipe his brow.

"What do you mean Señor Gonzalez?" Sara asked, suddenly very focused. "What do you mean, 'not again'?" Sara and I could hardly breathe, standing in the bright sunlight of a cloudless sky. We didn't want to miss a word of whatever Mr. Gonzalez was about to tell us.

"A few years ago, the same thing happened in Fortin Nuevo. I can't believe my son could be so cruel. He raped her in front of her two-year-old son. And now this," he explained, looking down at the ground. The man's shame and sorrow were palpable, and I could see Sara was deciding whether or not to continue questioning him. Thankfully, she asked one more question.

"What was the woman's name?" she asked softly, not wanting her question to bring more pain to Mr. Gonzalez.

"I don't remember her name," he started, "but her husband is the Judge in that town. Go there and you will find him. I am sorry for your trouble with my son," he continued. "He was always a disappointment," and he turned to walk back into his house.

Sara and I stood in mute astonishment. Then suddenly she called out. "Señor Gonzalez, may I ask you one more thing before we go please?"

He turned and said, "Yes, go ahead."

"How many years did your son complete in school?" she asked.

"Solo completó segundo grado," he answered, and Sara said under her breath to me, "He only went to second grade. He's probably illiterate in any language, Spanish or English."

"Thank you, again, Señor, for your time and information," Sara said, and we both turned to walk back to the truck, glad we had already packed to go home. We were on our way to Fortin Nuevo.

21

Tracking

I T WAS DARK BY THE time we got to Fortin Nuevo, a sizable town of maybe three to four thousand. We stopped at the first hotel we saw. It wasn't as nice as our previous hotel, but it would do, especially since we planned to only sleep there for the night, get up and find the husband of Gonzalez's previous victim, the Judge. Before we went to sleep, I talked over my plan with Sara.

We need to convince the Judge that his wife could help in getting Gonzalez to trial. "I don't know how long ago this happened, but even if we can't get him to Texas and he is tried in Mexico, surely a previous offense would add time to his sentence," I reasoned. She agreed and we continued to go over the way we wanted the conversation to go. "There's one more avenue we can try," Sara offered.

"I know the mayor of Chihuahua City," she said, "and if we could make the time, we could arrange to meet with him on our way home. What do you think?"

"Yes! Let's leave no stone unturned," I agreed. "We'll get up early and try to talk with the Judge as early in the day as possible. We're only about three hours away from Chihuahua. We can stop and see the Mayor if he has time, and then head home. With any luck, we could be back by 6:00 or 7:00 that night."

She agreed and we both drifted off to sleep. I woke up a few hours later to the sound of a rooster crowing, and checked my watch. Unable to get back to sleep, I finally got up, took a shower and got dressed. Sara did the same, and by 7:00 we headed out to find a restaurant.

Brainstorming how we could best get in touch with the "Judge" we decided our best bet would be to go to the municipal police station and inquire. Surely, they would know where his office was and, if we were lucky, maybe have a phone number. If we could accomplish anything by phone, we'd get home even faster.

By 8:00 the police station was crowded, but when two blonde women walked in, a sort of hush fell over the office. One officer walked up and very politely asked if he could help us.

"Yes, please," Sara said, "We're looking for Judge Campos. Can you tell us where his office is, or give us a telephone number for him? We have only a short while to stay here, and we need to reach him."

"Of course," the officer replied, "I can give you the phone number and also direct you to where his office is. He is sometimes very busy, so I don't know if you can speak to him today, but you can try."

"Thank you so much," Sara gushed, "you have been so helpful!"

We doubled back to the hotel to use our telephone in the room. It was quieter there and we could relax and not feel so rushed. We waited until 9:00, then dialed the number.

His secretary answered and Sara politely asked if she could speak with the Judge. "I am from out of town, actually from the United States and I don't have a long time to be here. It would be very helpful if I could speak with the Judge this morning if he has time," Sara continued.

The secretary asked her to hold for a moment while she checked to see if Judge Campos was in. He was, and the secretary connected him to Sara immediately.

"Thank you so much for speaking to me, Judge Campos," she began. She gave her name and began telling him why she was calling. At the mention of the name, Refugio Gardea Gonzalez, Judge Campos became agitated and angry.

"I understand he attacked your wife," Sara continued, "and I am very sorry for that. It seems that this same man came illegally into the United States, and he has attacked another woman. I know this is painful, but can you tell me what happened in your wife's attack?" she asked diplomatically. "I am looking for information that may help the woman he attacked in Texas. He is still in jail in Ojinaga, and I don't know if he will ever come to trial in Texas. But wherever he is tried, any information about his prior offenses could possibly help us."

Obviously trying to get himself under control, the Judge spoke in measured sentences. "He raped my wife in front of our 2-year-old son. He also had a knife and cut her severely during the act. That was almost five years ago. Both my son and my wife still have trouble sleeping."

"Judge Campos, I am so very sorry to hear of this. I know it must have been devastating for your wife, your son, and for you. Please accept my condolences. I hope your family is healing," Sara offered. "I hate to bring this matter to your full attention, but I must ask you just two more questions, if that is all right with you."

The Judge said he also had limited time, but she could go on with her questions. He followed that with, "But be brief."

"Yes, sir, Judge, I will," Sara replied. "First, I need to know if he went to trial for this crime and if so, how much punishment did he receive. I assume he went to prison," she said.

"Yes, he did go to trial almost immediately. He is a stupid man, on top of being cruel and heartless. "He did five years in prison," the Judge answered.

"This next question may be a little more difficult to answer, Judge, but I am compelled to ask. Would you and your wife, expense free, be able to testify at his trial, either here in Mexico or in Texas, so the court will know this is certainly not his first offense?" Sara paused, then went on to add, "It could make all the difference at this trial. He MUST come to trial somewhere, and face justice for what he has done. The woman in Texas also has a son, and this deed has all but destroyed their lives. I'm sure you understand."

"NO!" Judge Campos all but shouted, "I will not allow my wife to take the stand to again and again go through all the horror of that event. She is just beginning to heal."

"But, sir," Sara started, "It would be so helpful ..."

"No." he said again. "I'm sorry I cannot help you but my wife and my family must come first. We definitely will not come to his trial. I may kill him myself, if I ever saw him again. And I really must get off the phone now, I am very busy. I am sorry for what has happened to your friend, and I wish her well. I'm sorry I cannot help you. Please do not contact me again about this matter." And with that, he hung up the phone.

With fallen hopes Sara relayed what the Judge had said. "Well, we gave it our best shot," she said. "Everything works out the way it's supposed to," she continued, "whether we believe it or not."

I agreed with her. "You couldn't have argued a better case. I don't blame him for not wanting his wife to go through all that again. It's painful enough to live it, much less talk about it," I sighed. "Let's get out of here and go see the Mayor of Chihuahua City."

22

The Mayor

WE ARRIVED IN TIME FOR rush hour in Chihuahua. Tired and hungry, we pulled into the first nice restaurant we saw. Sara began calling Señor Gomez, the Mayor. Finally, after several attempts she reached his office and requested an appointment for later in the evening. After giving her name to the receptionist she was immediately put through to the Mayor.

Talking like old friends, he said of course he would meet with us. He was already familiar with the situation, but didn't have all the facts. "We'd like to fill you in on everything that is happening," Sara said, "and specifically everything that is NOT happening."

He asked for us to meet him at 7:00 that evening in his office.

"No problem," Sara answered, "We'll be there."

When she hung up, I realized we would need to stay one more night in Mexico. The roads at night in Mexico are treacherous, and we were already tired. "What the hell am I doing in another country," I thought. "I have about $500 to my name and here I am chasing after *someone* to help me bring prosecution against this man. He sits in jail and has meals brought to him on a tray and sleeps soundly," my thoughts continued down the "pity party" road. I decided I wasn't hungry after all.

Sara ordered a meal of fajitas, and I picked at the chips and salsa, too worried and anxious over meeting Mr. Gomez and what he might say. "I hate having to go through the whole story again," I said to Sara. "I hope he already knows enough so that we can just ask for his help in extraditing Gonzalez back to Texas. I really don't want to go through the whole thing again."

Sara assured me that Mr. Gomez was very polite and that I could speak to him myself, as he spoke almost perfect English. "If he wasn't willing to try to help you, he wouldn't be meeting with us," she said trying to ease my anxiety, "and also, he's a gentleman."

We finished eating and by 6:30 had found a nice hotel to check into. Leaving our luggage in the room, we drove the short distance to his office. Getting there was easy ... finding a place to park was a nightmare. The entire plaza in front of his office was teaming with people, and we had to park several blocks away. The PRI party headquarters was located on the ground floor of the same building, and there was a convention or something going on. Sara and I waded our way through the throng of mostly men, and tried to look confident and self-assured, as if we belonged there. Eventually we were spotted by Mr. Gomez's assistant, Reuben, and he waved for us to come up the steps to the second floor.

He led us down the wide hall and knocked on the door of Mr. Gomez's office. The knock was quickly answered by a strong, "Come in," spoken in English. Already standing behind his desk, Mr. Gomez walked around and shook hands with me and warmly embraced Sara. They spoke for a minute in Spanish, renewing their friendship, and then Sara started speaking rapidly, going over some of the details of why we were there.

"Wait," Mr. Gomez said, "let's speak in English. It will be easier."

He seemed a little bit pressed for time, and a little bit irritated at Sara's not-quite-perfect Spanish.

"Great," I thought, "I can handle this. Sara may speak Spanish, but I understand the subtleties involved in what I am here for." My eyes opened wide, I made sure I was "sitting like a lady", with ankles crossed, and making eye contact with the Mayor. I made sure my voice was calm and soft. Mexican men tend to place women into two categories, virgins or sluts. I didn't want to be seen as a slut.

His gaze settling over me, he asked how he could help.

"I want to see this man brought to trial," I began, "preferably in Texas, but if extradition is impossible, then here in Mexico. This is at least his second offense. He assaulted a woman in front of her child years ago and did some prison time for that. I want him to pay for what he has done to me, but since I am a foreigner, I am afraid that a trial in Mexico may not bring the justice I want. Can you help me get him extradited to the United States?"

"I believe I can probably help you," he stated. He seemed to be formulating his next words carefully and slowly said: "I can help you legally, or we can do something else". He stared at me intently to see if I understood.

I did understand and was quick to reply, "I want him to go to trial. I need your help to get that accomplished."

His eyes looked sorrowful and he began to apologize for the entire Mexican race of men. I replied, "It happens everywhere, unfortunately, and not just by Mexican men, but I thank you for your understanding."

"I think I can help you," he said, "and since you are staying in Chihuahua for the night, I will call you later at your hotel and give you all the information that I can find."

Sara handed him a note with our hotel and room number. I thanked him profusely, shook hands, and we left. Reuben again guided us through the lobby, and even walked with us the several blocks to my truck. We drove directly to the hotel and waited.

Just after 10:00 our phone rang. Mr. Gomez apologized that it was so late, and said that he didn't have much information. He had found out, though, that Gonzalez was still in jail in Ojinaga, and had not yet been formally charged. He had not been moved to Chihuahua as had been rumored. He went on to say he would eventually be tried in a Mexican federal court. He finished by saying, "Call me on Saturday. I will have more information by then." I thanked him and told him I would call him the following Saturday, making a mental note to get the tape and written statement of my account from Sheriff Jones. "At least I can try to have some input at his trial, even if it is in Mexico," I thought.

Now I *was* hungry, but was too tired to care. I dropped into bed and slept.

The next morning, we ate a hurried breakfast and started the trek back to Ojinaga, the border, and Alpine. I decided the trip had been somewhat successful. Getting to meet Refugio Gonzalez's parents had been enlightening. And the information from the Judge would certainly help at trial, if there ever was one, and if the court would allow third hand information to be admitted. And certainly, the talk with Mayor Gomez had been productive, with a promise of more to come. I felt hopeful.

Finally arriving back in Alpine, I dropped Sara off at her car, with promises to have lunch together in a few days. I called Steve's house and made arrangements to pick Noah up after school. I thanked them, and offered to have Steve stay with us if they ever needed a "get-away".

All commitments having been met, "Now there is just enough time to go home and have a quick nap," I thought, "before I pick

Noah up from school." I was exhausted and grateful to have the apartment all to myself.

But sleep didn't come. My mind whirled with thoughts of the trip, thoughts of what Mr. Gomez might say on Saturday when I called, thoughts of what a trial in Mexico would be like. And, of course, thoughts of my dwindling bank account. I could see no option other than to move back to my house in Terlingua. "At least it is paid for," I thought, "and I can probably pick up some part-time work somewhere."

Unable to sleep, I finally got up and started to unpack. Back in my familiar surroundings, I started to try to take my mind off the whole sordid affair and begin to be normal again for Noah's sake. After being gone, I was anxious to see him again and needed to put on my "best face". I had to constantly remind myself that I needed for him to feel that any upheaval was only temporary. I needed for him to feel safe. I needed to help him believe the world was a safe place, even though I knew it wasn't. He was just a child, and unfortunately would learn soon enough just how cruel life could be. I needed him to believe that like all American movies, everything would always eventually turn out all right. I needed to believe it myself.

23

A Twisted Turn of Events

THE FOLLOWING SATURDAY I CALLED Mayor Gomez several times, but was never able to reach him, and never able to even leave a message. "One more dead end," I thought, regretting the time and money I had spent on the trip into Mexico.

I had definitely decided to move back into my house in Terlingua. I had given notice to the apartment manager, and started to pack a few of our things. Noah was sad to leave his new friends, but eager to get back and ride his dirt bike again. I fairly drifted through the few remaining days I had in Alpine, spending my time packing, seeing Dr. Sanchez, and tying up loose ends.

I had promised to have lunch with Sara, and as I was walking to the small sandwich shop, I was stopped by an old friend and fellow school board member. She was also the daughter of one of the law enforcement deputies. Radiant, smiling from ear to ear, she pulled me aside on the sidewalk and sort of whispered, in a conspiratorial tone, "Aren't you AMAZED?" she asked, followed by, "Did you ever think this would happen?"

"I guess I would be if I knew what you're talking about," I answered. "What's going on?"

She stepped back and now had a different look on her face, a troubled look. "Well, ah, I thought you knew," she stuttered. "I'm so sorry, I thought you knew. Just go on over to Sheriff Jones and talk to him. I can't say anymore and I've already said too much. You need to talk to him." And she turned and quickly walked away.

My heart trying to beat through my chest, my thoughts racing a mile a minute, I switched directions and walked over to the Sheriff's office. The deputies inside were all smiles, and one of them said, "Sheriff Jones wants to talk to you."

He opened the door to the Sheriff's office and said, "She's here."

"Come in, come on in!" the Sheriff rang out.

I sat down and, hardly able to contain himself the Sheriff said, "We got him! We got him!"

"What?" I blurted out. "When did this happen? How did you get him across the border? Where is he now?" So many questions came spilling out of my mouth.

"First," he said, "look at these pictures. Point out the man we've been waiting for. I need for you to make a positive identification." He spread several photographs of men in front of me. It was easy to pick out Gonzalez. "That's him," I said, pointing to one of them.

"Great!" the Sheriff responded. "Let me tell you what happened."

"One night last week, I think it was Saturday, I got a strange telephone call. The person who called told me there was a naked man wandering around the roadside park on Highway 118. You know, the little park just past the Woodward Ranch on the east side of the road."

"Yes," I answered, "I'm familiar," flashing back briefly to the summer with Trey and how we would clean up the park every time we had a few spare minutes, not believing how tourists could be so careless. Actually, the land had long ago been part of the

Woodward Ranch, and had been gifted to the county destined to become a small park, under beautiful cottonwood trees.

"Well, I didn't have a deputy on duty who could go with me, so I just drove out there by myself. Really, I was thinking it was a prank call or something. No one just wanders around naked!"

"Well, was he there, like the caller said?" I asked, "Just standing there, waiting for you, or what?" I was incredulous at the whole story.

"Actually, no. And he wasn't naked, he had on a pair of underwear. He was trying to crawl into the metal culvert that runs alongside the highway. My headlights shined right on him. At first glance I thought he looked familiar. By the time I pulled him out of the culvert and handcuffed him, I had a feeling that it might be our man. I asked his name and he said, 'Refugio Gardea Gonzalez'."

"Last week? This happened LAST WEEK?" I asked, my voice sounding like I was spinning out of control. "Why didn't you tell me? Why has he been sitting in your jail for days? What the HELL, don't you think I deserved to know as soon as you apprehended him?"

The smile began to fade from the Sheriff's face and he looked confused, and, not used to being talked to this way, not sure how to answer me.

"Do you have any idea what it's like to think the bastard may reappear at any moment? Any idea of what it's like to vacuum your house wearing your gun on your hip? Can you imagine locking every door and window in your house before you go to bed, EVERY NIGHT?" I yelled, surprised to hear my own voice talking so boldly to our SHERIFF. "If I had known he was caught maybe I could have had a moment's peace. Maybe I could have stopped thinking about him coming back to finish the job," I said, in a lower tone, and trying not to cry.

With recognition now on his face the Sheriff got up and walked to the chair next to me and sat down. "I am so sorry," he started, "so very, very sorry. No. I didn't think of all of those things. I had no idea, no idea." And I could see he meant every word of his apology.

Embarrassed now, I, too, apologized. "I'm so glad you got him," I stammered, "so relieved that maybe all of this is coming to an end and I can get my life back. But how? How did he get back to Texas?" I asked, now realizing that there was more to the situation than just the Sheriff finding him in the park.

"I'm not exactly sure, but I'll tell you what I know. I'm sure there is more to the story than I've figured out so far. But, like they say, I know a little, and I can guess the rest. The most important thing is that he's back in Texas now, and we can bring charges against him. There will be a lot more information to come out, especially tomorrow in the Ojinaga newspaper. I spoke with El Presidente Municipal of Ojinaga. He called me to tell me that three masked men with machine guns broke into his jail in Ojinaga. It was around 2:00 am and at that hour the jail was guarded by only two jailers. The masked men wanted only Gardea Gonzalez, and one jailer took them to his cell. He opened the cell and they tied Gonzalez up, took him outside the jail, and threw him into the back of a pickup truck. The jailers described the men as being two Americans and one Mexican. They wore camouflage uniforms and had machine guns. There were no shots fired, but the jailers stated they were in fear for their lives."

I could hardly believe what I was hearing. "Do you know who did this?" I asked the Sheriff.

"I have no earthly idea," he said, "and if I did, I certainly wouldn't tell anybody. There is no statute of limitations on kidnapping. When I arrested him, he kept blabbering about 'Mexican Mafia,

Mexican Mafia.' He's back in Texas fair and square and we're going to prosecute him to the full extent of the law. How he got here isn't any of my business."

"So, what's going to happen now? Can Mexico demand we extradite him back to Mexico? I mean, it's an international border. Can any federal agency in the United States demand we send him back? This isn't going to be an international incident, is it?" I asked, now fearful that for some reason he'd be ushered back to Mexico before we could bring him to trial.

"It's already an international incident," the Sheriff answered. "My phone's been ringing off the hook. *The Washington Post*, CNN, ABC, all those reporters have somehow got wind of this deal. Let me offer you a little friendly advice. If I were you, I wouldn't talk to any of those reporters. They have a way of either putting words in your mouth, or twisting your words to say things you never would have said. Steer clear of 'em, that's my advice."

As I began to realize that this new turn of events would bring new problems as well, I felt a rush of returning anxieties. My talk with Sheriff Jones over, I thanked him, apologized again, and left. My emotions were all over the place. Glad he was back in Texas. Worried about the trial. Sad to be back in the "news". Happy I could go back home, knowing he wouldn't come after me again.

"I WILL get to have my day in court," I thought. "I WILL get to face you and watch you get what you deserve." I hadn't been this hopeful in months. I should have guessed it wasn't going to be that easy.

24

Just a Victim

THE MOVE BACK TO TERLINGUA was relatively easy, and Noah was happy to be back with his old friends again. It wasn't exactly that way for me.

Most of my "friends" I hadn't seen in months. I had previously resigned my school board position and was still on leave from the post office. I got mixed feelings from people I had known for years. I noticed that guys would sometimes hold my hand too tightly and too long, their eyes seeming to search for my reaction. My girl-friends, too, acted a little weird, avoidance being their primary mode of dealing with the awkwardness. Most businesses didn't want to talk about it, certainly not LaKiva where Gonzalez had been employed, even though he was illegally in the United States. The big resort on the river followed suit asking employees to keep silent about it to any tourists who inquired. So much was happening around me I didn't have much time to ponder on the why's of such behavior. I chalked it all up to "oh well".

As soon as word got out that Gonzalez was back in jail in Alpine, my phone rang off the hook. My good friend and EMT, Ann, kept a close check on me, and offered to take calls when everything became overwhelming. The Sheriff kept me up to date on whether he thought we would go to trial or whether Gonzalez would plea bargain. It varied from day to day. The people and politicians in Ojinaga were irate over the jail breakout, and some of those bad feelings were shared by people in South County. The river may be a physical boundary, but not a cultural one. People on both sides of the river had friends and family on the opposite side. People being people, many felt the need to agree with Texas law enforcement or sympathize with law enforcement in Mexico. And an uglier understanding was beginning to haunt me.

Some people actually thought I had something to do with Gonzalez attacking me, thinking that in some way I "provoked" it. It was never said out loud to me, but word gets around in a small, small town. That brought on more panic attacks for me.

"What if we go to trial and they find him INNOCENT!" I worried. "That's happened before. They call it a 'he said, she said' situation. What if the jury doesn't BELIEVE me?" and all the variations of that theme swirled within me.

Finally, Gonzalez was arraigned and appointed an attorney ... the best attorney in Alpine and probably Brewster County. Worried sick that he would manage to somehow get Gonzalez found not guilty, I called the Brewster County prosecutor. To add insult to injury, he was "too busy" to speak with me. I told his secretary that I would like to go over the case with the prosecutor and asked for him to please return my call. A week later he still hadn't called me.

I called again, stressing that I wanted to have input to the case by acquainting him with exactly what had happened. His secretary dutifully took my messages, but he never returned my calls. I heard that the prosecutor had not won a single case he had tried in Brewster County, and now he wouldn't even talk to me, telling his secretary to tell me he had listened to the tape of my statement

I had given to law enforcement. With the attorney for Gonzalez talking "vigilantism" since he had been unlawfully abducted from the Ojinaga jail, I was more worried than ever that his "rights" had been violated and therefore he would be sent back to Mexico. His lawyer stated the Texas court had no jurisdiction in the case, as Gonzalez was brought to the United States in violation of international law. Growing more concerned about the trial with every newspaper account I decided I had to take action of my own. I was not willing to leave my fate up to men I didn't know with this kind of power to impact my life.

I spoke with the Director at the Family Crisis Center and asked for advice. "Given the circumstances, Jayson, I would write the prosecutor a letter stating your concerns and requesting a special prosecutor be appointed for this case. If you want me to, I'll contact the National Organization of Women and I'm sure they would write a letter on your behalf, echoing your concerns," she offered.

My relief was instant. "Thank you so much!" I almost wailed. "I will write the prosecutor a letter, and I'll send a copy of it to you. If you want, you can include it in the letter you write to the National Organization of Women. Your support means so much to me," I added.

I mailed the letter, certified return receipt, the very next day. About 10 days later I got a response from the prosecutor, a very cut and dried response.

"Thank you for your interest in the State's case against Refugio Gardea Gonzalez," it started. "Since you are only the victim, you will not need to have an attorney of your own present. The State of Texas is your attorney." His words, "only the victim" sent me into a rage. I could hardly read the rest of the letter. "Your request for a special prosecutor to be appointed is denied, because ..." and I couldn't believe this part, "I do not need a special prosecutor."

Blinded by tears of pure rage, I spent the next hour rampaging around my house yelling obscenities, wishing every vile curse I could think of on the man. "Even my 11-year-old son has better reasoning capabilities than this moron!" I yelled. The very idea that he had the nerve to refer to me as "only a victim", and the temerity to think I would place my fate in the hands of a prosecutor with his sorry reputation was obscene. I could see I was getting ready to be victimized AGAIN. Only this time, there was no voice except my own to tell me what to do.

I called the Crisis Center again, and read the letter to the Director. She was as incensed as I was, maybe more. "He has just brought the wrath of GOD down on himself," she yelled. "I will now write EVERY women's organization and request they support you with letters and requests of their own! If you DON'T get a special prosecutor there will be hell to pay!" she added.

Buoyed by her energy and support, I decided to ignore the advice given to me by Sheriff Jones and speak to any and every reporter who contacted me. I would let them all know what kind of justice was in place on this remote Texas border. If a third-rate lawyer/politician got elected as prosecutor, it didn't mean the citizens would have to stay silent and put up with it.

As the whole "Incidente Gonzalez" became more and more public, reporters of every kind descended on South County. The nearest resort, Lajitas, where Gonzalez had crossed back into Mexico, was refusing to talk to anyone about it, other than to say, "We've lost 4 tourist busses last week alone! We don't want people to think there are rapists hiding under every bush out here!" This story was bad for business.

The man Gonzalez was working for, Gil Feltz, had the same reaction. Hiring illegals was no big deal, and he needed the help to build the rest of his RV park and bar, La Kiva. Gil and I had been friends for years, and to his credit, he just refused to talk to anyone about any part of the incident, hoping the whole story would die a quick death.

With local news publishing every turn in the case the story grew bigger. It didn't help that the April edition of *The Washington Post Magazine* published a frontpage article, with a picture of the stark desolation that was South County. That was all it took. CNN followed with a television crew and their own coverage. By July, even *Playboy Magazine* had a piece about "vigilante justice" in its "Forum" section. It featured a poor man on his knees, blindfolded and handcuffed to a drinking fountain. Titled "Border Justice" the short article went on to say there was speculation that the American men who had kidnapped him out of the Ojinaga jail were, "friends of the victim".

I was furious. "So much for truth in journalism," I thought. "No wonder people look at me like I'm some kind of freak. If I had friends that could do something like that, I'd be afraid of me too," I worried. With all the speculation about "who did it", the gossip mill was working full time. The trial had been moved on a change of venue order to San Angelo, away from the "border type atmosphere" that both the prosecutor and public defender agreed would be the best for all concerned. A much larger city than Alpine, it was still basically a farming and ranching community. "Good," I thought, "salt of the earth people. People who won't tolerate things of this nature. Decent people who haven't heard all the hype, gossip, and innuendos."

The trial was set for early August. About 3 weeks before it was scheduled to begin, I was notified that a special prosecutor had been appointed. The new prosecutor was female, and from the Harris County District Attorney's office. Harris County is Houston, and with experience like that my fears of Gonzalez somehow getting off scot-free lessened. With letters of support coming from the National Organization of Women, Gloria Steinem, and other women's advocacy groups, the Special Prosecutor, a woman, was more than excited to take the case. She contacted me by telephone, and I liked her immediately. We made arrangements for her to come to Terlingua to meet with me and hear everything I had to say. She also wanted to get a better understanding of the "last frontier" as South County was called, to be able to include a perspective on the area that the jurors could understand. "They will most likely think that you should have called 911, or that you could have run to a nearby home or business to get help. Once I've shown them pictures of this area, they will understand perfectly well what a horrendous event this was for you. Every law enforcement officer I've spoken to has reinforced the fact that you only survived because you were smart enough to outwit him. And, I might add, brave enough to jump out of a moving truck and flee to safety."

When she arrived at my house, days later, I couldn't have been more pleased. She was young, yes, but I could tell she was hard-nosed when it came to criminals. None of the namby pamby "I had a hard childhood" crap would make a dent in her stern demeanor. She was a prosecutor. And to her, I was obviously more than, "just a victim".

25

The Trial

THE DAY BEFORE THE TRIAL began, I left Terlingua to drive the three hundred and twenty-five miles or so to San Angelo. I wanted to get a good night's rest and be calm for the next day's court proceedings. Calm? Hell, I was a nervous wreck. Jury members had already been selected and the actual trial was to begin the next day. The prosecutor met me in the hall and directed me to a small office behind the Judge's seat in the courtroom. "You will be the first witness called," she said, "so be ready. Just answer all the questions as honestly as you can. When his attorney cross examines you, don't let him make you angry. Keep your composure. Just remember everything we've talked about and be yourself. Let us lawyers do the work."

I was glad for the lawyers to do the work. What was the hardest for me to do was to tell the story, again, and in excruciating detail! I would be telling the most horrendous and embarrassing things to an entire room full of strangers – both women and men. I would be using correct anatomical words to describe what he had done to me. It was ghastly.

The prosecutor left to go out to the courtroom, and I sat alone, trying to compose myself. Refusing to let all the "what if"s storm my brain, I simply prayed. "God, please help me now to say the right things. Please keep me focused on the questions and not on my feelings. I put everything in your hands, Father God, for your outcome will be the right one." It wasn't long before I was called into the courtroom.

I took my seat in the witness stand, raised my right hand and swore to tell the truth and nothing but the truth. Glancing at the jury I could see there were maybe 5 women and the rest were men. No one was smiling.

There was a display of photographs on several easels, showing what Terlingua looked like, and showing my house. I had no neighbors and the stark terrain left nothing to anyone's imagination. The place was isolated, rocky, and vast.

In front of me, maybe 5 feet away, sat a stern looking Refugio Gardea Gonzalez. He had on a brown shirt, and wore a necklace with a large wooden cross on it around his neck. He never took his eyes off me. A tattoo on his arm said, "Fanta". I hadn't noticed it during the events of that hellish night and now I wondered what it meant.

The prosecutor started by asking me if I saw the perpetrator of my attack in the courtroom, and if I did, to point him out. "Yes," I said, "It's the man sitting there in the brown shirt, staring at me." The translator sitting next to him repeated my words to him in Spanish. He quickly looked away.

The prosecutor went on, watching me for any signs of distress, as she said she would. Thankfully, she asked the questions and, most of the time, I only had to answer or elaborate. Horrible, embarrassing, personal questions answered in a room full of strangers. Overwhelmed, I started to cry. "This is the last thing I wanted that bastard to see me do," I said to myself. But the stress of the courtroom, and the recounting of those horrible events were simply too much. The prosecutor paused and handed me a tissue.

The room was deathly quiet. Struggling for composure I finally nodded that I could go on.

Every question, and my every answer, was translated for him. The jurors looked from me to him, and back again, all of them listening intently. Finishing her questioning, she sat down and it was the defense attorney's turn.

He started his questions by introducing himself, and stating that he was not going to ask me any "trick" questions or try to embarrass me. "We only want to present the facts and the truth to the jury, and I'm sure you want the same thing," he said. His words sounded kind and I began to relax and focus on what he would say next.

He handed me a list of clothing items I had worn the night of the attack. "Take a look at the items you were wearing that night. Take your time and tell me if the items listed here are exactly what you were wearing that night."

I carefully studied the list, wondering what he was getting at. "Pink corduroy jeans, T-shirt, bra, socks and pink and beige boots," I read to myself several times. "Yes sir, yes I believe that is exactly what I was wearing," I stated.

"Then can you tell me why there is no underwear listed in the items? Do you usually go without underwear? What kind of woman walks around with no underwear on? What were you getting ready for to happen?" he continued, his voice growing louder and louder. "So much for being kind," I thought.

"No sir," I answered, my voice showing my obvious surprise. "I always wear underwear. But I had been in Alpine for 2 days. I wore underwear going there, but I had forgotten to pack a clean pair. So, the next day I decided to go without rather than wear the pair I had arrived in the day before." I was embarrassed to have to go into such detail about my underwear of all things, but it was the truth.

He asked more questions, and some required me to say the words I dreaded, and describe the acts that were so shameful. I'm sure my face was red the entire time. Finally, he was finished and I was dismissed. The bailiff ushered me back into the little room, and out the side door into the hall. The judge had called for a short recess and the hall began filling up with people coming out of the courtroom. I sat down on one of the benches and watched the hustling and bustling of people going to the water fountain, restroom, and generally milling around. The special prosecutor came out and told me that I had done a fine job on the stand. She congratulated me on my composure and told me not to worry. I was astounded by what she said next.

"You will not be allowed to be in the courtroom during the rest of the trial," she said gently. "I'm sorry, but that rule is in place so that the jury isn't swayed by being able to see the alleged victim while the trial is in progress. I know it sounds ridiculous, but really, it's the best thing for you, too. What if he gets on the stand and lies through his teeth and you get really upset? What if you lose your head and say something from the audience? And one more thing. If he is found guilty, and he will be, and appeals to a higher court, he can't say the jury was influenced by you being in the courtroom. It's really the best thing."

I was astounded. I wanted to know every lie he told. I wanted to hear every excuse he or his lawyer made for his sickening behavior. But after she had explained the reality of the situation, I could see the merit in the rule.

Friends had come from Alpine to see the trial, and reporters, most of whom I knew by now. I realized I could rely on them to tell me what went on in the courtroom. One girlfriend said she would take notes and give me a blow by blow account. I had to be content with that, and so I sat on one of the benches in the hall throughout the trial.

There were others in the hallway, too. A reporter from the San Angelo paper flitted in and out, eavesdropping on any conversation I had. A representative of *La Raza* was there making disparaging remarks about me, unaware that I was the victim.

"She just wanted to see what sex with a Mexican was like," she hissed.

I stared at her long enough that she finally turned around to look at me. "You are simply wrong," I said, and moved to another bench.

True to her word, my friend came out to report the courtroom drama to me during recesses. The interesting part was when Refugio, himself, got on the stand to give his side of the story.

"He was asked by the prosecutor what the tattoo, 'Fanta' on his arm meant" she said. "It's a soda water in my country", he answered in a quiet, almost childish voice. The prosecutor didn't let that stand and retorted, "No, I believe it means PHANTOM, doesn't it? PHANTOM, as in MONSTER, right?" she pressed.

"Sometimes," Gonzalez meekly answered.

She went on. "When asked why he was wearing that big wooden cross on his necklace, he replied that you were a WITCH, and he wanted to protect himself. That brought a chuckle from the jury," she finished.

I knew exactly why he thought I was a witch, a bruja. "He must have seen something, too, when the voice told me to forgive him," I thought. "His eyes were big as platters and he had a startled look on his face. I wonder what he was seeing, hearing. "No, you jerk, I'm not a witch. I'm a child of God and He protected me," I thought.

"Then Billy Pat got up to testify," she went on. "He reported that he had never heard a victim with such a clear recall of what had happened," she said. "He went on to say, 'Everything she said was exactly what the evidence showed. The strips of the poncho he tied her up with were found over the edge of the arroyo. We knew she was blindfolded as he dragged her through the desert because his footprints went around cactus and catclaw, while hers went through the stuff.'" Billy Pat was also a pilot and had his own small plane. A tracker for many years, he added: "I know he took her to that mountain because by air I could follow the footprints ... they shone like new money. We found the twig of greasewood and a cigarette butt in her jeans pocket, just like she said, and we matched the dirt under her fingernails to the claw marks in the dirt where he first raped her. Funny thing, though. She didn't have dirt under the fingernails on her right hand, but we figured out why. On her back while he raped her, she dug into the dirt with her left hand. But we found fist marks where her right hand would have been. She unconsciously pounded the ground with her right fist. Not only physically torn in two, she was psychologically torn in two."

"Billy Pat's testimony was awesome, Jayson," she continued. "You could see several jurors actually wince when he described what your hands were doing. It's like part of you, your left side, was conscious and wanting to put evidence under your fingernails, while your right side was unconscious and caught in the horror of what was happening. The jury got it," she finished.

"I think the court is going to adjourn for the day soon," she reported. "If so, they will re-convene in the morning, my guess is at 9:00. But I'll let you know."

She was right, and within the hour the court adjourned. My friends and I went out to eat that evening and Trish, the special prosecutor, joined us. She thought the trial was going well, and said that the jury would probably recess tomorrow morning after closing arguments. I was glad to have the company and to not have to think about what the jury would decide. My peace of mind was in their hands. My reputation was in their hands.

The next morning, I drove to the courthouse early. By 8:30 the hall was again filled with somewhat familiar faces, but the woman representing *La Raza* was not there. By 9:00 most of them had filed into the courtroom. I sat in the hall.

Evidently the closing statements by both attorneys were brief. At 11:00 the jury adjourned for deliberations. I wasn't hungry so I didn't join my friends for lunch. Besides, I didn't want to leave the courthouse. I waited in the hall, and listened to other people talk about what they thought the jury would do. By now, most of them knew who I was, so nothing unkind was said. I spent my time trying to read the San Angelo newspaper and pacing the hall. At 3:00 the bailiff came out into the hall and announced the jury was returning. He instructed that I could now come into the courtroom to hear the verdict.

I had heard people in the hall say that a short deliberation by the jury surely meant that they had found him guilty. Others weren't so sure, reasoning it could just as well go the other way if the jurors were tired and wanted to go home. I figured a 4-hour deliberation would be in my favor. I was about to find out.

I sat in the back of the courtroom among my friends. The jury filed in and confirmed that they had reached a verdict. The judge ordered the room to be quiet while the verdict was read, and demanded that there be no outburst of any emotion when the verdict was heard, citing his ability to hold in contempt of court anyone who disobeyed his orders.

A hush fell over the room and the jury foreman stood to read their verdict. "Guilty on all counts, your honor." The jury had taken 4 hours to reach their verdict.

I had not realized I had been holding my breath until I heard the verdict. Tears silently streaming down my face, I let out a sigh of relief, burying my face in my hands and sobbing quietly. The judge thanked the jury and instructed them to leave. He announced that the sentencing would be at a later date, to be determined, and remanded Refugio Gardea Gonzalez into the custody of the Brewster County Sheriff.

I walked into the hall and was surrounded by friends, law enforcement who had worked so hard on the case, and well-wishers. Everyone was ecstatic. We all made plans to meet at a nice restaurant later in the evening and celebrate. Walking out of the courthouse, reporters were waiting on the steps, all of them asking for comments. I thanked everyone I could think of ... the people of San Angelo, the court, the jurors, law enforcement, and all the friends who had stood steadfastly by me. I said I was moving on with my life. I was.

At sentencing, Gonzalez received a prison sentence of seventy-five years.

26

Moving Again

THE TRIAL WAS OVER, BUT the after effects of the ordeal were still in full force. I still could not abide loud noises to mask other sound. I still had bouts of depression that I had to take medicine for. I still flinched if anyone came up behind me. I was still a mess.

Feeling like I could no longer live in Terlingua alone, I had resigned from the postal service. I needed to figure out how the rest of my life was going to be. Again, good friends came to the rescue. The Peppers, my old bosses from the Vila de la Mina, had moved to their small central Texas hometown. I rented a house there, and enrolled Noah in school for his 7th-grade year. The tiny town of about four hundred people was a safe place to be, and I gave myself that year to rest, recover and decide what to do next.

I told myself I had nothing to do but heal for the next several months. That would be my work. Answers would come. A direction would appear. All I really needed to do was to be Noah's mom and put myself back together.

After everything that had happened, Noah was thriving. A young boy of almost teenage years, he wasn't sure of who he should be. Coming from Terlingua to another small town seemed like a very big deal to him. The first day of school he dressed in a suit and tie. I was afraid the other kids would make fun of him, but just the opposite happened. They adored him. He was elected to the student council. He loved his school and teachers. Life for him was good, except now he had a hovering mother who had time to monitor his every move.

Still riding his dirt bikes in the surrounding fields kept him busy. But I caught him one day trying to go riding without the proper gear, mainly a helmet. We argued. We shouted. I demanded. I insisted he put on a helmet before he left or he wasn't leaving at all. He groused. He pouted. Time running out, he finally agreed to wear his helmet.

Twenty minutes later I had a phone call. "Mam, this is Uvalde Emergency Services calling about your son," the voice began, "to let you know he has been in an accident. He's going to be okay, but he does have some broken bones. Please meet us at the hospital." I thanked him and rushed to the hospital about 15 miles away.

Several broken bones and a very bruised ego kept Noah in the hospital for a few days and with a broken pelvis, he was in a wheelchair for several weeks. "Thank God I made you wear your helmet, Noah," I said a hundred times. "If you had gone without it, well, let's just say we wouldn't be having this conversation." We never had to argue about proper gear again.

That experience taught me a valuable lesson. Even if you're in the depths of despair, even when you think you can't possibly do, or feel, or think another thing, life doesn't stop.

All the activity of life does not stop because you think you can't handle it. Life goes on, whether you "handle it" or not. It's not what life hands you that is so important. It is how you respond to what life hands you that defines you.

I realized I had to figure out a way to raise my son and go on with my life. The sooner I made the decisions on how to do that, the better I was going to feel.

Now that the trial was behind me, I started the long journey to climb out of my year-long depression and commit to getting my life back in order. I was so at a loss of losing everything all at once, home, job, security, friends, and the road back seemed insurmountable. And of course, there was the mystery of "the Voice".

I remembered the words that directed me that night over and over in a never-ending loop. Dr. Sanchez had had no answer for me about that. My new counselor in a neighboring town, had no answer. My own questions never brought an answer, only more questions. "Was it God? Was it the Stockholm Syndrome? Was it ME? Was it a guardian angel? Whatever 'it' was, it had kept me alive, and now it haunted me like a specter. Still on anti-anxiety medication, I spent most days sitting and thinking, running the events of that night over and over in my mind – an endless loop with never any answers.

I realized I needed to be in an institution of some kind. I felt like I was either going crazy or I was already there. I would have some clarity until Noah was off to school, then take my medication and spend the rest of the day going over everything, bit by bit, sitting in my favorite chair and, like a child, trying to put all the pieces of my life back together. By the time Noah returned home from school, I was present enough to make him a snack and talk a bit about his day, trying to feign some semblance of interest. At night I lay in bed still going over the horrific events. Still trying to figure out the Voice. A couple of months of that and I finally surrendered. "Yep, I'm crazy. I belong in a padded room somewhere," I thought.

After going over all the alternatives, college seemed the best and most viable choice of institutionalized care. I had about 2 years of courses left to finish the degree I had started right out of high school. "I could still have Noah with me, I could prepare in some field to get back to work, I could be focused on something else, and I could buy some time to heal," I reasoned. And with that decision, my choices slowly started to take shape.

I had two years of college credit from the University of Texas from earlier years when I lived in Austin. If I finished my degree my chances for gainful employment increased tremendously. What kind of employment would offer the most freedom in where I lived? I wondered what kind of employment would be a benefit to the world? What did I like? What did I hate?

I set about making lists and answering just such questions. For the next several months I gathered information and resources. Texas had set up a department called Crime Victims Compensation. In concert with the Texas Rehabilitation Commission, these entities provided some services for victims of violent crimes. I applied.

After certification of my ordeal, and several interviews, I was accepted to have books and tuition paid for, as long as my grades were passing and as long as I took at least 12 hours a semester. That financial help, along with the traditional government grant per semester, and my own savings, added up to twenty-four months of financial availability to go back to college and finish my degree. That was exactly the amount of time I figured I needed.

Now that I knew I could afford it financially, I was plagued with other questions. How would Noah adapt to yet another move? Was I too old to go back to school? Would I be able to do the work? Was I dedicated enough to put my full focus on my education? What if I couldn't do the work?

I decided I had to try. After everything I had already been through, surely, I could put up with two years of college, I reasoned. Now the question became, which university? I didn't want to have to live in a huge metropolitan area, like Austin or San Antonio, but I wanted to be in the University of Texas system. At the time, that left El Paso. And even though I had some horrible memories of far-west Texas, I also had some of the best memories of my life. I missed my desert. Finally, my mind was made up. I would move to El Paso and attend the University of Texas at El Paso.

I decided I wanted to become a teacher, and planned to major in English and education. There were many reasons for picking this track. My work hours would coincide with Noah's school, I could work anywhere, and I would have the chance to impact children's lives in a positive way. Maybe education would stop another Refugio from emerging.

I began making plans to move to El Paso. Noah wasn't happy about it, but I told him that in the long run it would be the best for both of us. And I reminded him we would only be three hours away from Alpine and Terlingua, and he could visit his friends.

After school was out in May, we packed up our furniture and other belongings in one of Pepper's trailers and a rented U-Haul, and began the trek to El Paso, some ten hours away. I was terrified. I had never pulled a trailer before. The weather wasn't helping by dumping torrential rains in the area. In fact, our little entourage of movers were the last vehicles to cross the river near Uvalde. I was driving about 15 miles an hour. My friend, Ann, was driving the U-Haul, and Billy Pat, who by chance was on his way to El Paso anyway, was driving his pickup truck, loaded with my stuff. He pulled over and ran through the downpour to my window. "Have you ever pulled a trailer before?" he asked. When I said "No," he said, "We won't get to El Paso until sometime next week at this rate. Let me drive your truck and trailer and you drive my truck," he continued. I jumped at the chance. And finally, we were on our way to El Paso. Someone once said, "At the exact moment of completion, a new journey begins." They were right.

27

And Again

EL PASO WAS A CITY, albeit a small and manageable one. I found a new counselor and met with her every week. She, too, had no answer as to what the Voice was. I began attending a church and met with the pastor. Hoping to gain some understanding of what had guided me that night, I asked for his best guess of what the Voice was. Again, no answer. I was beginning to understand that this quest for an answer to that mystery was mine alone. I would have to come to my own understanding and acceptance of who, or what, the Voice was. As I became involved in my new life, the urgency of that question began to recede.

I started school that summer, and loved it. My classes kept me busy and that was just what I needed. I continued to see a counselor, and some the symptoms of PTSD were starting to abate. After two semesters at the community college, I transferred to UTEP on the far west side of El Paso. Noah and I moved again to be closer to campus, and that fall he enrolled in high school. He hated it.

Teenage years are hardly bearable for anyone, even when everything is good. When you have had chaos for several years, switched schools, lost friends, those years can be horrendous. They were terrible for Noah. I tried everything I could think of to make things better for him, but the deep depression that began in those years lasted until his 30s. He still refused to see a counselor. Another casualty of Refugio G. Gonzalez.

We both missed our friends in Alpine and Terlingua. We missed the wide-open spaces of the desert, the Milky Way. I missed the ranch and I missed Trey. I stayed in touch with his sister, Emily, and brother, David. I had been contacted by Emily, as she was divorcing her husband. She finally told me that her husband had a violent temper and had threatened so many times to kill her. More than that, the abuse had gone on for years. She was scared, and with two small children, she was thinking she needed to get away. But more than scared, she was defiant. "Why should I let him make me leave my home?" she asked. "He's the one who needs to leave!"

I tried to convince her that the best thing she could do would be to relocate, at least for a while, until the divorce was final. "After the divorce is final you can go back home," I reasoned. "I'm betting a change of scenery would do you good. You can live here with me and Noah. We have a big house and there's plenty of room for you and the kids." After she went into detail about the way her husband treated her, I was more than scared for her.

"Well I could probably just stay here and get a restraining order," she countered. "It would be a lot less hassle. All my friends are here, not to mention my job," she finished.

"But I WANT you to come here," I begged. "You won't need a job, just be with your kids and get the divorce done. Come ON ..."

"I'll think about it," she said, and we went on to talk of other things. During the course of that conversation she told me that Trey had married, and a baby was on the way. The memories of the ranch and the summer Trey and I spent together flooded my thoughts. I had always thought that somehow, sometime, the magic of that year would be ours again, when the time was right. Now I knew that it would never be. I was glad for him that he had found love and moved on. But as for me, I felt enveloped by the emptiness that comes when a cherished dream vanishes. Now I had lost everything, even Trey.

It wasn't long before I heard from Trey's brother, David, and it wasn't good news. Emily had been murdered by her soon-to-be ex-husband ... shot to death in broad daylight on the streets of Alpine.

I couldn't believe it. Sweet Emily, the little girl I had taught to play the guitar that magical summer. The daredevil cowgirl who tried to out-do Trey with horse tricks. My conversation with David was short as we had both dissolved into tears. He managed to tell me when the funeral would be, and we hung up. I fell into a depression so deep I couldn't make myself go to the funeral. I wanted nothing more to do with the violence of the border. I was angry with God and I was angry with life, and I was fed up with trying to find answers to things that didn't fit. I couldn't wait to be somewhere else, anywhere else, away from this border. The light of my adventurous spirit darkened, and I buried myself in my course work, hoping to graduate in record time and get the hell back to the civilization I once knew.

Two years went by, and by the time I graduated, desperately broke, I accepted the first job I was offered. In the Ysleta school district, the job was a 5th-grade class in the suburb of Horizon, on the east side of El Paso. We moved again, this time to a small town near my school, about 15 miles away. It would be an easy commute. Noah enrolled in the high school in that town. I prayed for an uneventful year, a chance to earn and save some money, and an opportunity to leave the border completely by the end of the year.

But by the end of that school year I had decided a person would have to be insane to be a teacher. I had never worked so hard, and so long, for so little, in my life. With a classroom of forty-three 5th-graders and no aide, it was exhausting. The first year of teaching is always the hardest, and I knew that. But I had no idea that after teaching all day, doing lunch duty, bus duty, after school faculty meetings, grading papers at home at night, writing lesson plans and a million other duties, there was precious little time to be really involved with your students. This was a poor school and many of my students were first generation to even go to school. There were language problems. Many lived in the colonias surrounding the area with no running water or electricity. They arrived at school hungry too. They all needed so much more than "just" education. With Noah's ongoing depression and my schedule, by the end of the year I was exhausted.

I didn't renew my contract and we took the summer off and headed to California, via the Grand Canyon. I had heard that California schools paid much better, and with my sister living there, I thought I could find a job teaching and a change of pace for Noah. We spent time camping in the Grand Canyon, but not nearly enough. I was anxious to get settled in California and find a job.

Spending a summer in California was enough to show me that maybe teaching in Texas wasn't such a bad idea after all. The California traffic was unbearable. The cost of living was sky high. You had to drive miles and miles to find any rural country, and then it wasn't satisfying because you still had noise and smog. Maybe it was just me. I'm not a city person, and didn't want to learn to be. I decided to leave. Noah stayed, and enrolled in a community college near my sister's home. I went back to Texas to find a smaller school district, and one located off the border.

The following three years I found myself teaching in a much smaller school district in North Texas. I flourished there, but the climate was horrible. Flat, hot, snow and ice in winter, wind storms that often became tornadoes, I finally gave up and accepted a teaching position in central Texas. Located in a small but growing town, all the advantages were there and few disadvantages. The district was medium sized, my 4th-grade class was under twenty-four students, and I had a part time aide!

I had hit my stride as a teacher. I loved it now and all the challenges it brought. But in time it was obvious it just wasn't quite enough. Long ago I had taken a job as a school secretary. After I had moved to Terlingua, I became a member of the local school board. On each occasion I was thinking I could help kids and schools. I became increasingly aware that today's children bring almost insurmountable problems with them to school. Their home lives are often devastating. They are often poor. They are often victims of one kind or another. "To really help kids," I thought, "I should be a school counselor." The counselors were my heroes. After all, counselors had helped to fix my own broken life not so long ago. I had watched them work in every school I had been in. They were usually first to hear a child's outcry. They helped to fix families in trouble. They helped kids. I started to dream of going back to school for my Master's Degree to become a counselor.

And with time, my feelings about Brewster County had mellowed. I missed my friends. I missed the everyday easiness of life in the Big Bend. Every day away from Brewster County brought a little more ache to my heart. It's hard to describe how a geographical location can become a part of you, the biggest part of you. When one first arrives in Alpine, or Terlingua, or Brewster County in general, people say you either love it or hate it. The stark reality of desert life, of being a part of "The Last

Frontier", either fills you up or scares you off. I missed it in one way or another every day for ten years. I began to realize I had to get back. A plan emerged.

Alpine has a small university that serves a good portion of West Texas. It began as a teachers' college a century ago and its education department offered classes in various disciplines for teachers to obtain higher degrees. And, best of all they offered these classes on weekends. I began to formulate a plan where I could get back to Brewster County, work as a teacher during the week, and attend classes on weekends to get my Master's Degree in Counseling. After 8 years of teaching, 1 year to deal with the trial, 2 years of living in El Paso, and yearning every day to be back in Brewster County, I had found a way to get back to the home that had been so violently ripped away from me. At the end of that school year, I put everything in storage and headed for Alpine and "The Last Frontier" of Brewster County. I was happier than I could remember being in years. At long last, I felt I was going HOME.

28

Alpine Strong

THE DRIVE BACK TO BREWSTER County was a sight for sore eyes. From central Texas and its crowded roads and cities into the vast stretches of lonesome vistas, I felt my spirits lift the closer I got to Alpine. My favorite vista is coming down Highway 67 from Monahans, just before you reach Interstate 10. Both sides of the road are framed with small hills and the middle of the road opens up to your first glimpse of mountains. The misty blues, lavenders, and purples form a picture-perfect view of the landscape. I couldn't help but say a loud "THANK YOU, GOD!" for bringing me safely back to where I knew I belonged. The place that had attached itself to my heart so many years ago. The first place in my adult life that had felt like "home".

I stopped at my favorite motel and got a room for a week. Sparse but clean, with vinyl floors and good beds it was right across the street from Sul Ross State University. I was anxious to sign up for summer classes, and the next day I spent most of the day getting my classes straight, doing paperwork, and buying the books I needed for the first session. Sul Ross University sits on a hill overlooking Alpine and as you stand on the old administration building steps your eyes are drawn to the length of the town and the breadth of the county. You feel as if you can almost see Marfa, some twenty-five miles away, and the Davis Mountains to the west sit like silent sentinels guarding the whole area. I felt like the winner of some grand prize, standing there, surveying the whole spread. "How did I get so lucky?" I asked myself. "How had all my previous choices and experiences added up to this gift?" As I thought back on all of my life changing experiences in this astonishing and majestic place, my whole being felt at peace. I knew I had made the right choice to come back.

I wasn't sure if I still knew anyone in town, and I wanted to share with someone that I had been accepted into the Master's program and was now back in Alpine. I knew that Barbara was still in Brewster County, but she lived in Terlingua, and I wasn't ready for that trip yet. Knowing I would probably regret it, I decided to call my father.

I hoped that he would be thrilled that I had made such headway out of the darkness of 10 years ago. In his defense, I suppose he wanted only the best for me, and for me to be away from any memories full of heartache. But that's not the way he sounded. It is such a hard, and sometimes defeating struggle ... going through the stages of life with a parent. My father was old now, and changing so quickly he might as well be a young child. Is it only in the beginning and the end of our lives that we change so rapidly? Is it the long middle that lulls us into thinking we are immortal? I don't know. All I know is that it is very difficult to be fifty years old and still someone's child – and to be eighty-three years old and still be someone's parent.

My father is his own contradiction. Needy and aloof, he seems to dare anyone to come too close. And if you manage to somehow scale the walls of his own prison and touch him, you feel immediately rejected. He is a master at rejecting you in the very terms you have come to see yourself as. If you are kind, he mocks your kindness. If you are smart, he denigrates your intelligence, letting you know that he assesses intelligence to be a deadly sin. He seems to tell me with every look that he is both bored with my very being, and incredibly lost by himself.

He no longer remembers certain words in everyday conversation, but is quick to tell you he always remembers numbers. And he always does.

My father says openly that almost everyone he ever knew is now dead, and so refuses to make new friends. He is so fragile, and yet believes he can hold at bay the changes that are coming. Here in the last stage of life, he doesn't want to let go, and yet doesn't want to go on. He wants things to be the way they were ... the way they were before he knew he couldn't control everything in the universe.

Perhaps it is seeing your child enter yet another "new" chapter of her life. Perhaps he is envious that my world involves forward movement and his own movement is only marching in place.

My father was not overly happy to hear from me.

"What? You're going BACK to school AGAIN?" he asked. "Don't you ever get tired of doing that?" he continued. "And WHY in God's name are you back in Alpine? After everything that happened, couldn't you find a safer place to be?" he scolded. "And just how do you intend to pay for this?" he added as his final reproach.

"Don't worry, Dad," I answered, "I'll be fine. Alpine is one of the very safest places to be, and I won't be living anywhere near Terlingua. The good news is that I can continue teaching during the week, and go to school on weekends. After teaching these last few years, I really think that counseling would help so many more kids. It's something I've thought about for the last couple of years and I've saved a little money so I can pay for everything myself. I'm not asking you for money, I just wanted to let you know where I am," I finished, hoping he could see this as yet another step in my healing.

I told him I would let him know as soon as I got a new job and we ended our conversation with the usual, "Love you, Dad", that he would only echo as, "You too."

I spent the next two days interviewing for a job in Alpine. The weekend arrived with no plans in sight. Not knowing who was living on the ranch, I decided to drive out and say hello to whoever was now "holding down the fort".

Passing Cathedral Mountain took my breath away. I had to stop on the county road to just sit and stare at it. It looked slightly different. The mild earthquake of 1995 had toppled an overhanging cliff of rock on the north face. Other than that, it was the same view Trey and I had looked at as we went to different parts of the ranch. I felt so grateful to have had that summer with Trey on the ranch, and to have been a part of his family, however brief. It still felt like home.

I finished driving the two miles or so and got to the ranch house. It looked so much the same, I almost felt like I was in a time warp. Getting out of my car and walking up to the ranch house, a woman came walking across the yard, asking, "May I help you?" I didn't recognize her and assumed she was working on the ranch, and thought I was a tourist or a rock-hound. "No, I'm just a friend of the family and stopped by to see who was here and say hello," I answered, reaching the kitchen door and knocking. "Well I think Trey's asleep right now," she said, as I stopped dead in my tracks. "Trey's here?" I asked, now worried I would intrude on him and his wife. "Trey and his wife were living in Midland, the last I heard," I continued, "I wouldn't want to bother them."

"Oh, they were divorced several years ago," she said, "Trey's been back managing the ranch for a couple of years now."

I swear my heart skipped a beat when I heard her words. All the old memories flooded my thoughts, followed by all the typical fears of reuniting with a lost love. "Would he remember me? After I left the ranch and he stayed, was he still angry with me? Would he even want to see me again?" Now I was unsure if I should even go in. "I'm an old friend," I managed to stammer, "but maybe I should just call first."

"No, in that case go on in. He shouldn't be passed out on the couch in the middle of the day, anyway," she laughed, and turned and walked away.

The smell of alcohol led me to the couch in the living room. Sure enough, Trey was stretched out, dead to the world. I touched his shoulder and said, "Trey, wake up," as gently as I could. He opened his eyes and called me by the nickname he had for me. "JAYSON! Is that you?" he said as he jumped up from the couch. And then, "Oh God, I must be dreaming!" as he grabbed me and held me like he would never want to let me go. Finally, he held me out in front of him and said, "Let's fix some coffee and get caught up."

As the morning wore on, he said, "Come on, we'll drive over to Seven and talk there by the creek. It'll be cool under those cotton-woods and it's the perfect place to spend the day."

"Seven" was the name for the east side of the ranch. Different from the west side, this part of the ranch had beauty of its own. Ash Creek cut through the sections, and it was much more remote ... wild, with no buildings anywhere on it save the old pens near the front gate.

We loaded up into his old pickup and drove out to the highway, then south the few short miles to the other side of the ranch ... Seven. When we passed the small roadside park where the Sheriff had picked up Gonzalez after he was brought back from Mexico, Trey looked over at me. "Still the same little park," he said slowly and cautiously, with a wide grin starting to spread across his face. Without another word we both broke out laughing.

Driving through the ranch gate and the two miles or so to Ash Creek, we bounced along the dirt road just as we had years ago. Talking about nothing, counting cows, we crossed Ash Creek and pulled up under the cottonwoods. We got out and sat on the tailgate of the old truck and started to recount the years that had gone by, like the two old friends and long-lost lovers that we were.

I asked him about his marriage. "It was the wrong woman at the right time," he said. "I really didn't know her very well. I was lonely. I guess she was too. I was in jail for another DWI and she came to visit me. As it turned out, Papa liked her family ... her father was a bird colonel and he was pretty impressed with that. We got married and before we knew it, she was pregnant. I went back to work in the oilfield to make some money. We had a little boy," and his voice trailed off to a stop. He looked away but I caught a glimpse of tears in his eyes.

"What happened?" I asked softly.

"He died," Trey almost whispered before giving into long held back tears. "It was all so wrong," he blurted out. "The whole thing was just wrong. We divorced within three years. He and his mother lived in Alpine, so I got to see him a lot. He was hit by a pickup while riding his little bike when he was 7 ... just a tragic accident that nobody was ready for. How could anyone be ready for something like that? Another tragedy for the Woodward family. The last few years have been really rough. With Mark's suspicious death, and Emily's murder what's left of my family is in pieces. It didn't help that Papa went through a divorce with his second wife. Whew ... what a mess."

I was crying now, too. "Trey I am so very, very, sorry. When I didn't hear from you for so long, I had no idea it was because things were so sad. If I had known about your son, you would have heard from me. When Emily died, I was in such a bad place in my own life. I was still so mad over the kidnapping and rape, I couldn't bring myself to come to the funeral. I'm sorry ... so sorry."

"Well, things weren't going that great for you, either," he said gently. "I knew I couldn't call you or do anything after what you went through, but I thought about you constantly. I wanted to find the guy and kill him, myself. But the way things worked out, I guess that was good enough. For him to be kidnapped after kidnapping you, well, like they say, Karma's a bitch."

"I heard a rumor that after he was kidnapped, he was held on some ranch for over a week," I said, watching for any reaction from Trey. "I don't know who broke him out, but whoever it was, I'll be eternally grateful to them. I'm glad it went to trial in Texas. I wanted everyone to know it wasn't a 'he said, she said' deal. I had never seen the guy in my life, and I certainly wasn't involved with him in any way other than being his random victim. Whoever got him back to Texas is my hero. First for doing it, and second for not just killing him so that no one would ever know the truth of what happened."

Trey had a slight smile on his face as he looked silently off into the distance. I had seen that look on him before, a look that told me he was wrestling with some decision. I held my breath, expecting some revelation. But when he spoke again, he turned and looked straight at me with those incredibly vibrant blue eyes and said, "That's all in the past, so let's leave it there. We've both been through so much. I should never have let you leave the ranch to begin with ... none of this would ever have happened. I've always blamed myself for that," and his soft smile faded to tears again.

"Don't blame yourself, Trey. *Life is life and shit happens!* That IS life. We never know what's coming at us, and you can't prepare for something you didn't know was going to happen," I said as we both sobbed over lost love, lost youth, lost opportunity.

We both cried until it got ridiculous, then laughed at ourselves. "Good grief," he said, wiping his eyes, "That's enough of that! Let's drink a beer and you tell me what you're doing back here in the Big Country."

We talked until late afternoon, when he said, "Come on, let's go get your stuff. You're not staying in a motel, you're staying at the ranch until you find a job."

"Well, I don't know, Trey, do you think that's a good idea?" I asked with some hesitation.

"What do you mean?" he answered emphatically. "You need an address, a phone, a place for your stuff until you get settled. Of course, it's a good idea. No strings attached," he ended, sensing I was worried about some attachment neither one of us was ready for. "You know there's a spare room, and it's all yours."

"What about Frank?" I asked, "he's not gonna like this at all."

"Frank's in El Paso living with his girlfriend. He never comes back to the ranch and I'll make it clear he has no say in this. Things have changed, Jayson. He's not in good health, and he leaves me alone to handle the ranch the way I see fit. He won't be a problem. I'm sorry he ever was," he explained.

The offer made sense, as I had three other school districts to contact for a job, all of them miles and miles apart. The ranch would be a good central location, and I could come and go as need be. Besides, I was so glad to be back in touch with Trey again I couldn't think of a better way to get reacquainted with each other ... a little bit at a time.

Within a month I had a teaching position in Presidio, the small town on the border with Ojinaga. It wasn't my first choice, but it was a job. I rented a small apartment and left for central Texas to get my belongings out of storage. Trey helped me move everything to my apartment in Presidio and offered to let me stay at the ranch on weekends to attend classes at Sul Ross. I was one step closer to resuming the life I had wanted for the last ten years. I was back in Brewster County, I was getting my master's degree, and I was back in touch with Trey. Things were getting back to "normal".

29

Back Where We Started

TEACHING FULL TIME, I WAS only able to attend Sul Ross on a part time basis. I loved my two classes, and knew I had made the right choice. I would teach my 4th-grade class all week in Presidio, drive back to the ranch on Friday afternoons, and attend classes at Sul Ross all day Saturday and half a day Sunday. Then drive back to Presidio late Sunday afternoon or evening. It was a busy schedule, but, almost, everything I wanted.

The school district in Presidio was grueling. After teaching for ten years, if there was one thing I had learned it was that your building principal could make or break your teaching experience. The best principal I had ever worked with was in central Texas. He was always on his teachers' side, battling the battles that often come from administrators. He made the four years I taught there not only a valuable experience, but a beautiful memory.

That wasn't the case in Presidio. Faculty meetings called on the spur of the moment that lasted past 6:00 pm, rooms with no air conditioning, a campus ill equipped for the little 4th-graders I taught, added up to some very unpleasant experiences. By the first of November of that year, I had had enough. I resigned.

Trey was ecstatic when I told him. "I'll come down and help you move everything back to the ranch," he practically yelled. "You'll stay on the ranch with me."

"I can't, Trey," I said with a heavy heart, "I just can't."

"What? Why not?" he demanded. "What is wrong?"

"You're an alcoholic, Trey," I tried to say as gently as I could. "I can't stand to watch that. You're killing yourself in slow motion. I can't be a part of it," I said sadly. "I simply cannot be around a person who is drinking himself into an early grave. I love you too much."

There was a long silence on the phone. And then, "Well I'll quit. I'll quit right now. I'll never touch another drink," he said emphatically. "I love you. I want you here on the ranch with me. Believe me. I'll quit."

"You will? Really?" I exclaimed, "You'll do that for me? For yourself?"

"I will," he promised, "I'll never touch another drink."

The week before Thanksgiving Trey brought his big trailer and a couple of buddies to Presidio to move everything I had. Classes were over for the Thanksgiving break, and together we spent the following week unpacking and planning a Thanksgiving feast for all our friends and tourists on the ranch. And, true to his word, Trey had given away or thrown out everything with alcohol in it. But within a couple of days, he was really sick.

I hadn't had enough experience with alcoholics to know that, if you have been drinking most of your life, you shouldn't just quit on a dime. And with just a semester of counseling classes under my belt, I hadn't studied alcohol and chemical dependence yet. We cancelled Thanksgiving dinner that year, and Trey struggled to get better.

I sat with him day and night, bringing cold wet cloths, making sure he was hydrated, and keeping his drinking buddies at bay. I made bland soups to give him some nourishment. I worked in the rock shop and handled the tourists. I gave him time to heal.

He confessed that probably the scariest part was not hanging out with his friends ... his drinking buddies. He worried that he would have no friends. The truth was, his drinking pals weren't his friends. They used him to buy the beer, they used the ranch to hang out in their drunken stupors. All of that had begun to change as soon as I moved in, and slowly the people Trey thought were his "friends" began to disappear. I found out later those "friends" had given me a new nickname; "Wicked Witch of the Wanch". That was fine with me, as long as they left Trey alone. And just as I had predicted to Trey, new people began to show up. People who were interested in the geology of the ranch. People who loved the serenity of being in nature. People who genuinely liked Trey.

And as the days turned into weeks and the weeks into months, Trey began to change. He was interested again in building up the ranch. Together we updated the rock shop, adding a new ceiling and lighting. We stayed busy cleaning up outside the shop, where all the loose rock was kept for people who bought in bulk. He started working on the yard, turning it into a green oasis and bringing back to life the beautiful grass, the yellow roses his mother had planted, honeysuckle vines and peach trees that had long been neglected.

Classes resumed in January and I had enrolled full time for the spring semester. One Saturday Trey and I had been in town shopping for groceries and running a few errands. He seemed a bit out of sorts, anxious.

As we drove down the county dirt road going home, he suddenly told me to stop the car. "What?" I said. "Right here? What's wrong?"

"Just stop!" he all but yelled.

I pulled over, turned off the truck, and we sat silently looking directly at Cathedral Mountain. I waited to see what he wanted.

Fumbling through his pocket, he pulled out a diamond ring. A ring that had been his mother's. Shaking and almost out of breath he asked, "Will you marry me? Will you just make me the happiest person on earth and finally marry me?"

Surprised and shocked, of course I broke into tears. "Yes, I will," I said, and then we both cried and held each other as we sat there looking at the magic of Cathedral mountain, remembering who we had been together these many years, with and without each other, and joyous at the prospect of many more to come.

And with those sweet words the long journey of pain and loss, uncertainty and doubt, fear and mourning just faded away. We had come full circle, unknowingly making the choices that seemed right, the choices that would lead us back to the beginning of our true spirits. Now, we were both "home".

Epilogue

THE NEXT FOURTEEN YEARS WERE the happiest years of my life, and I believe, for Trey also. But in 2011 Trey was diagnosed with late stage cancer, and three days later he died. His ashes were scattered on his beloved Woodward Ranch and his spirit rests there still. Getting through those days after Trey's death are chronicled in my first book, *The Heart Remembers: A Memoir of Personal Growth*. His memory is cherished and lives on in the hearts of all those who knew and loved him.

The Texas/Mexico border and far-west Texas remain just as dangerous now as it was then, some thirty-odd years ago. The danger now, however, is muddled with political correctness and a country divided by talk, not truth. And it is now further complicated by the world-wide phenomenon of refugees from failed states, desperate to find a new home. Under cover of darkness, those who cannot wait to enter the country legally walk through the desert, pass retirement communities and homes of urbanites who are "living the dream" in far-west Texas and other border communities. Many residents of the beautiful Chihuahuan Desert are unaware of the danger that passes, unseen, beside them, down their roads, through their pastures, and, occasionally, through their homes. Today the tourist trade has grown to heights previously unimaginable, and no one wants to strike fear into the hearts of those who offer a financial lifeline by publicizing any sort of dangerous situation. And no one wants to be charged with racist rhetoric by the social justice warriors of the day. And so, the danger festers silently with few openly talking about it, and little, if any, news coverage.

But the danger is, indeed, real, and the knowledge that our county, still the largest in Texas with over 6,000 square miles, has only six deputies to offer a modicum of safety, has led some to begin to become responsible for their own safety. And after Trey's death, I became one of them. There has been a surge of women's groups to educate women and girls in the use of firearms for their own protection. A local chapter of the national organization, The Well-Armed Woman, is large and growing. Every offering of classes for license to carry a firearm is filled. The local shooting range, hosted by the Big Bend Sportsman Club, has a huge membership not seen in the past, especially a surge in female members. There are classes and seminars teaching how not to become a victim, how to attain situational awareness in any environment. How to stay safe. The age of innocence of the "Land of the Last Frontier" departed long ago, along with the romanticism of the early pioneer days.

They say there are stages to becoming competent in being accountable for yourself and for your own protection.

At the first stage you are *Unconsciously Incompetent.* You drift along in a sea of imagined safety, sure in the knowledge that safety is something that someone else will provide. It's the "move along, everything is fine," mentality. You don't know what you don't know.

If you're lucky, as I was, to have some incident shake you out of your complacency, you may become *Consciously Incompetent.* You become aware that, should the worst happen, you would not have a clue what to do. You would undoubtedly become a victim should that circumstance arise.

Hopefully, that knowledge will spur you on to try to become *Consciously Competent*. You may begin to look for opportunities to learn and apply behaviors that will keep you safe should the worst happen. You will seek to gain the knowledge and training that will keep you from becoming a victim.

The ultimate goal is to become *Unconsciously Competent*. With enough knowledge, training, and practice, you can become confident that you can handle any emergency situation without having to guess what to do. Indeed, you will have no perceivable thought process when confronted with an emergency. You will simply react immediately and confidently. EMTs and first responders work hard to achieve this level of simply putting your knowledge and training to work in an emergency situation. Like them, you will have become, *Unconsciously Competent*.

There are many ways to improve your chances of survival should you encounter any number of emergency events. There are countless classes and seminars on how to survive an active shooter event. There are classes to teach effective techniques if you are in a struggle with someone who would do you harm. There are emergency medical classes that teach field techniques that may save your life or someone else's. There are classes and trainings everywhere that teach you how to safely carry and effectively operate a handgun.

Today's world can be a dangerous place, especially for females. If a woman survives an assault, sexual or otherwise, she has done the right thing whatever she did to stay alive. If she begs, bargains, pleads or acquiesces, and lives, she has done the "right" thing. But in my mind, it is better to be able to take control of a situation rather than give control to an assailant, who by the very definition, does not have your best interest in mind.

157

Any kind of trauma can be a precursor to PTSD – Post Traumatic Stress Disorder. After contracting this disorder, very, very rarely does it completely go away. It may lessen in severity and frequency, but it does not go away. The ripple effect will encompass your loved ones and friends, your children, your family. If you have practiced taking control of a bad situation, and feel confident in protecting yourself and possibly others, the severity of PTSD may be acute, but the lingering effects will probably not be as severe. You won't spend years second guessing yourself as to whether or not you "could" have done something different. You will be competent in ensuring your own survival, and possibly the survival of others.

The assault I suffered and relate in this book, happened to me years ago … when I was unconsciously incompetent. In the intervening years I have been fortunate to learn how to be more accountable to myself. I have taken steps to prepare myself mentally, physically, and spiritually to lessen the chance that I will ever again be a victim. It is my fervent hope that you never need to protect yourself from an attack, but that if you do, you are prepared and capable to defend yourself.

The seasons change, the times change. Political issues of the day swing back and forth, changing in intensity and speed. We live our lives in a long and twisting dance called life. We learn to swim in the waters of oblivion.

Acknowledgements

THE COMPLETION OF THIS BOOK would not have been possible without the help and commitment of many. I owe a huge debt of gratitude and thanks to Michael McDaniel for his expert help with today's technology, without which I'd still be using a pencil and a Big Chief tablet. Hearty "thank you's" go out to my sister-friends, Jan, Peggy, and Sally for reading early drafts; and to John for his early reading and comments.

The law enforcement officers who worked this case showed professionalism and kindness throughout the ordeal, and for that I am eternally grateful.

Many others played a major part in my journey or recovery and without naming them all, I say "thank you" for listening and caring.

And finally, a major and heartfelt thank you to Dixie Maria Carlton for her expert guidance, generous support and unfailing belief in me.

About Jayson Woodward

LEARNING TO NAVIGATE HER WAY through a dangerous and disintegrating family, Jayson Woodward has been writing and counseling in one form or another her entire life. Reaching adulthood, she went on to earn a B.S. Degree in Education and Writing, and then a M.Ed. degree in counseling.

She became a certified teacher and taught writing for ten years. She counseled young clients in a school setting over issues which she, herself, was all too acquainted.

"I believe books and writings of any kind that reach people can positively impact their lives" has been a mantra throughout her life. In *Borderline*, her second book, she hopes her narrative will inspire readers to overcome challenges associated with victimhood, while teaching basic information in defending against predation.

Her first book, *The Heart Remembers*, her numerous short stories and songs, all reflect the power of people, especially women, to overcome adversity with mercy and forgiveness.

A well-seasoned traveler, Jayson has lived near many borders: the southwestern border of the United States, Belize, Guatemala, Costa Rica and Peru. Her travels have served to broaden her interests in geology, gemstones and jewelry making and to enrich her understanding of life through cultures different from her own.

As a single mother to a son, she learned that wit and humor can go a long way to survival of almost anything. In fact, while trying to grow up in her birth family, comedy became one of her strongest coping skills. And so throughout her writings, the reader will sometimes come across humorous writings in the most solemn places. "Humor diffuses stress, and life is all about dis-tress and eu-stress. Laugh a little."

Currently Jayson lives in the southwest and continues to write.

www.JaysonWoodward.com

To request more information on how you can work with Jayson, or have her speak at your next event, please email: jayson@jaysonlwoodward.com

You can access Jayson's Author page via this link:
www.facebook.com/Jayson-Woodward

Be sure to follow Jayson's author page on Amazon or visit her website for details of her next book The Heart Remembers. *Due for release in mid-2019.*

Resources

RAINN - Rape, Abuse, Incest National Network
https://www.rainn.org
800-656-HOPE (4673)
National network for sexual violence, Safety & Prevention

National Domestic Violence
800/799-7233
https://www.thehotline.org

Stress Management Training
https://www.laurel-house.org

Wild Iris Family Counseling & Crises Center
https://wild-iris.org
877/873-7384

Victims' Rights - the National Center for victims of crime
https://www.victimsofcrime.org

https://www.fbi.gov/resources/victim-services/coping-with-
victimization

Refuse To Be A Victim
https://rtbav.nra.org
https://thewellarmedwoman.com/about-us/

Front Sight Firearms Training Institute
https://www.frontsight.com